Adam's Righting Revolutions

Adam's Righting Revolutions

One Child's Literacy Development from
Infancy Through Grade One

Judith A. Schickedanz
Boston University

Heinemann
Portsmouth, New Hampshire

Heinemann Educational Books, Inc.
361 Hanover Street   Portsmouth, NH 03801
Offices and agents throughout the world

Library of Congress Cataloging-in-Publication Data

Schickedanz, Judith A., 1944–
  Adam's righting revolutions : one child's literacy development from infancy through grade one / Judith A. Schickedanz.
    p. cm.
  Includes bibliographical references.
  ISBN 0–435–08511–5
  1. Language arts (Preschool)—United States—Case studies. 2. Language arts (Primary)—United States—Case studies. 3. Cognition in children—United States. 4. Early childhood education—United States. I. Title.
  LB1140.5.L3S33 1990
  372.6—dc20   89–49688
                                                        CIP

Designed by Maria Szmauz.
Photo on back cover by Marjorie Siegel.
Printed in the United States of America.

90 91 92 93 94   9 8 7 6 5 4 3 2 1

To Adam, who turned out to be a "paper and pencil kid"; to Dolores Durkin, whose inspiration during my school days at Illinois helped to ensure that he would be; and to Bernard Spodek, whose requirement of "put it in writing before we talk about it" got me into the habit of making notes to keep careful track of all sorts of things.

CONTENTS

PART   TWO   CONNECTIONS

A P P E N D I C E S

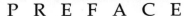

July 6, 1988, was a special day at our house, because it was Adam's seventh birthday. With this milestone came another childhood rite of passage: graduation to a youth-sized bicycle. The previous summer's smaller two-wheeler, with training wheels, was traded in for a bike that would accommodate longer legs, better balance, faster reaction time, and a more grown-up sense of self.

Because the bicycle was given to Adam about a month early (to take advantage of the first weeks of summer), falls and scraped knees were now behind us. Adam sat calmly, and very relaxed, on his bike, riding it with considerable ease and little effort. As I watched him go round and round an oval track in a nearby park, images of earlier times passed through my mind.

Adam's first ride atop two wheels was in a yellow seat attached to the back of his father's bike. Adam, strapped in and helmeted, literally went along for the ride, contributing nothing except, of course, a burden, given the weight, not to mention the worry, that his presence added. While it would have been easier to ride alone, it seemed right to take him along on these family outings. After all, he could do his part, which entailed sitting erect and leaving his helmet on.

Before long, Adam had some wheels of his own, first a small scooter, whose seat sat close to the ground right on top of four wheels, propelled by Adam's feet. Then came his first tricycle, which requires pedaling, but which solves the problem of balance by placing two widely spaced back wheels directly under the child's seat. Adam would have a total of three tricycles before he would leave them behind altogether. Each was a little larger than its predecessor, requiring a little more strength and giving, in turn, a little more speed.

Finally, there was the small two-wheeler, with its training wheels attached to the back. Until Adam had this bike, I'd always thought that training wheels touched the ground when the bike was sitting perfectly upright. But they don't. The wheels are raised a bit—perhaps an inch or slightly more—off the ground. They touch the ground only when the bike tilts toward one side or the other. Their design is intended to allow children a chance to get a feel for balancing a two-wheeler without suffering any harmful consequences. Adam righted himself dozens of times while riding the bike with training wheels. But he still wasn't home free. When riding his new bike without training wheels, he had to learn to right himself, which he did after a fair number of falls.

I am, by personality and profession, an observer and a keeper of notes. Adam has been an interesting subject. The story to be told in this book, however, is not about how Adam learned to right himself while coasting along on a bicycle. It is a story about how Adam righted himself cognitively many, many times as he learned how to write. There was a long period of apprenticeship, with supports equivalent to the scooter, the tricycle, and the bicycle with training wheels. Finally, there were the situations without much support, which demanded more of Adam.

Before Adam was born, I envisioned myself keeping notes about many aspects of his development. During his first year, I kept daily notes about his schedule and activities, and I started to document his interactions with books. But as time went on I underwent a little righting behavior of my own: I realized that time constraints would limit my ability to document Adam's overall development. If I wanted to capture an area in detail, I needed to narrow my focus.

Adam's markings—his drawing and writing—seemed suitable candidates for study. These spoke for themselves in a way that other aspects of his behavior did not. First, they existed in concrete form, on pieces of paper, which had backs—handy spots, as it turned out, for jotting a date and some notes. If there wasn't time to write extensive notes at the moment that a sample was created, it was easy to jot enough to provide sufficient context, given that the pieces themselves provided a basic description of what Adam had done. When I lacked time even to jot a date, a paper's position in the stack of papers, many of which were dated, preserved some vital information until I could look at them more closely.

Adam's markings also appealed to me because they could be observed from afar. Adam attended family day care, beginning at the age of two months.

Descriptions of his behavior provided by his care-givers were sometimes difficult to grasp in full detail. But with his markings, I had a record to help pre-serve some of the meaning of moments my own eyes had missed.

Finally, I chose to document Adam's writing development because of my professional interests. I had been interested in young children's literacy development since 1976, the first year that a colleague and I had received a grant to help teachers in day-care settings develop literate environments. In the meantime, I had grown weary of seeing development in limited one- or two-year school-based slices. I wanted to see literacy development over the long haul, from its very beginning to its end. (To me, the "end" was the point at which the behavior becomes fairly conventional—the point that marks the beginning for most people.)

This is how it happened that I collected Adam's papers and jotted down what I was able to learn about the context of their creation. But I did not know at first what I might eventually do with them. In the beginning, I wasn't even sure that I would use them for anything at all, except for enjoyment, of course, and perhaps to enrich a lecture or two in some class that I was teaching.

I enjoyed looking over these papers for several years, in the same way that one enjoys reading through a baby book or flipping through a family photo album. But I didn't search through them with a mind set that deserved to be called critical analysis. It wasn't until the summer of 1985—Adam's fourth year—that I took a long and careful look. Even then, however, nothing in particular struck me. I looked upon the samples as a collection of individual mark-ings. Progress in Adam's writing and drawing was evident, of course, but no particular pattern stood out.

Then, during the spring of 1986, I looked at the samples again. This was the first time that one part-icular pattern, the series of word-creation hypotheses that Adam had used, caught my attention. Perhaps it's only when we take a long look—a look that spanned six years, in this case—that we truly can see the magnitude of what a child's mind has been up to. Adam had been up to quite a lot.

The story told here focuses on just one aspect of Adam's writing development, on how he came to understand how words are made. The story begins with his first scribbles and continues to the point where he began to appreciate the complexity of our spelling system. In between these points, we see Adam give up the idea that symbols need to have a physical relationship to the things they represent, work hard to discover how words should look, and then abandon his concern about appearances as he gained insight into how words could be written by using letters to represent sounds. Then we see despair set in as he discovers, once again, that the way he thought was how you do it was not really right, after all. But he triumphs—rights himself—in the end, when he begins to appreciate the elegance of the system.

Adam's story is told through the writing samples themselves, as well as through notes that provide details about the context of his creations. If a marking had been made at home, these notes were based on my own observations. Because Adam attended the Boston University Preschool, where I serve as Director, I sometimes made notes there, usually from the vantage point of an observation booth. When my notes were not based on firsthand observations, they sometimes were based on the comments Adam made about a paper, either spontaneously or in answer to a question I posed. I also made notes when information was provided by his caregivers or teachers. Sometimes I asked these adults about aspects of Adam's behavior just the way any mother would. When what they told me applied to Adam's writing or drawing, I jotted it down. Sometimes a teacher, aware of my interest in young children's writing development, gave me a note or a letter that

Adam had given to her. This, plus the rich, literate environment of Adam's preschool, probably yielded a larger number of samples than might otherwise have been the case.

Though the writing samples and notes tell the basic story, I have augmented them in a section called "Comments." Here I explore how one writing episode or example relates to other episodes or to other behavior and how it appeared to me to fit in with what Adam was trying to learn and do. The "Comments" are my attempt to reduce the data, to bring the individual writing episodes together, to spin from them the strands of thinking—the hypotheses—that seemed to me to answer the questions "What was Adam trying to do?" and "Why was Adam doing what he was doing?"

The third part of the story is told in Part II of the book, "Connections." Here I reflect about the similarities between Adam's behavior and the behavior of other children, both those whom I have studied and observed and those whose behavior has been described by other researchers. I also reflect on the meaning of Adam's behavior for parents, teachers of children, teacher-educators, and researchers, all roles that I filled simultaneously watching Adam grow and learn.

Like any author, I often wondered who would read what I was writing. At different times, I thought my book would be primarily for one audience and then for another. I now feel it will be of interest to a variety of readers. Researchers who are studying the course of children's literacy development will want to read and study it. Many parents will find it interesting and useful. But many researchers are removed from children's everyday lives. They have an impact only via a parent or a teacher who puts their knowledge and discoveries to use. And by the time parents figure out what's going on, the child has grown beyond what the parent understands. But teachers get to go back again and again, with each new year and new class, to try to do a better job in their work with children. This is why I believe that teachers can make the best use of the story I have to tell, and why I have tried especially hard to write this book for them.

one

Adam's Story

I n Chapters 1–5, I trace one aspect of Adam's writing development: his underlying conceptions about how words are created. His first thought was that words need to look like the things they represent. Later, he accepted the fact that words look different from their meanings. Still later, he thought that written words should be related to the way they sound. His early idea about this relationship, however, was based on a system of syllabic coding, with marks selected at random from the repertoire he had at hand. In time, this notion also had to be abandoned, probably because words formed in this way (e.g., AO for Adam; OA for mom-my) don't look much like most of the words children see: They are too short.

Adam's next idea was that words need to look a certain way. He had a whole set of rules—criteria— by which he thought they should be judged. They musn't be too short or too long, and they musn't be composed by using just one kind of mark or letter. When finished creating one of these mock words (e.g., AOAO, OAONO), Adam often asked, "What word is this?" or "What does this say?" only to find that, nine times out of ten, he hadn't created a real word at all. This idea was also given up eventually, which left Adam thinking that he must learn the order of letters for each and every word in the world, which he set out to do. But in the process of gathering this information, he began to notice some patterns. He decided that there is a way to determine which letter comes next in a word: Sounds within words are represented by specific letters of the alphabet. There is a code of correspondence that one can use to generate words. Each one need not be memorized in isolation.

Having broken the code, Adam set out on a virtual writing spree. But despair set in when he discovered that his word for a particular object or person didn't look like the representations created by others. He was stumped until he realized that words aren't always spelled the way they sound and began to see why this gives the system an advantage.

We leave Adam at the age of seven, when he still has much to learn about writing—so much that those unfamiliar with the actual length of his total journey might think he had just begun. Only by watching Adam from the very beginning of his journey to literacy does it become possible to marvel at how far a seven-year-old has traveled and to give him the respect that he deserves.

Even so, I don't start at the very beginning. Before Adam's first attempt to make a word, he developed notions basic to writing. First, he explored marking tools themselves, and discovered that, when touched to a surface, they leave a mark, thus making a record of our movements. Second, he discovered that marks can be both repeated and varied. The variations appearing in Adam's first lines did not represent variations in meaning, to be sure, but the discovery of the potential for variation itself paved the way for the later idea that different lines can be exploited to serve a symbolic purpose.

During this early period, the idea that an arbitrary meaning could be imposed on different graphic configurations escaped Adam, but the idea that objects and patterns could be pictured did not. We see Adam discover the symbolic potential of lines as he noticed (quite by accident, I think) that some of his configurations resembled, and reminded him of,

objects and patterns he had seen in his world. Later, he noticed that the organization of the graphic displays known as pictures differ from the graphic displays known as writing: The former can be organized somewhat amorphously, while the latter must be organized very strictly. Later still, Adam realized that internal details of lines mattered too. If the graphics were to be considered writing, the lines must be composed of special marks—marks that resembled, or in fact were, alphabet letters.

So as not to give the impression that Adam's thinking about words, which emerged at the age of two years, eight months, appeared out of the blue, I've included in the appendix a record of Adam's marking experiences and development from the age of one year up to the point where Chapter 1 begins. There the reader can learn how much experimenting and thinking preceded the beginning of the main story: how Adam learned about words.

1

"Should My Name Look Like Adam or Sound Like Adam?"

Adam Discovers That Words Are Not Pictures of Things

At the age of two, Adam brought his concept of pictures to the writing arena. He had scribbled on paper since he was a year old, and he had experimented extensively on paper with various lines and shapes. He had discovered through these experiments that forms made at random sometimes resembled forms or patterns he had seen in the world. On these occasions, he was surprised and delighted that something he had created looked like something he knew about or had seen. Later, he discovered that he could set out to create a particular form, that he could represent something he had seen with marks created on paper. (See Appendix A for a more extensive discussion of this early development.)

It shouldn't have been surprising, then, that Adam's first written word—his name—was primarily a picture of himself, although the organization of his writing was not picturelike. In other words, the writing itself was organized linearly, the way writing is organized, but his *concept* of word-making, his hypothesis about the way people decide which and how many characters should be included in a specific word, was picturelike.

Adam chose vertical lines to serve as the characters in his name, and he tried to coordinate their number with his age. Adam might have chosen the vertical lines because they resembled the two fingers he raised each time someone asked, "How old are you?" If this was the case, there are two ways in which he pictured his name: by using a mark that resembled the way he showed his age to others; and by using the number of marks that corresponded to his age, which was two.

Names written with a picturelike hypothesis lack the arbitrariness that exists in the creation of written language. The very nature of written language as an abstract symbol system, one in which there is no physical relationship between symbol and object represented, escaped Adam at this point. But not for long. Soon, Adam began to try to write his name the way he saw others writing it, with specific letters arranged in a specific sequence. Apparently, he had accepted the arbitrariness of language: "If everybody says that this design says 'Adam,' then I will accept it too." It was during this period that he asked us to show him how to make several letters, including *A* and *M*.

At this point, Adam's concept of word-making was completely arbitrary and associative, without any generative rules. He assumed that each word had its own visual design that must be copied and learned. This visual word-creation strategy differed from a later visual strategy that was rule-governed and could be used to create a lot of "words" — *amod*, *moad*, *omad* — even though Adam didn't know which words he was creating ("What word is this?") or, in most cases, that he hadn't created a real word at all. Nevertheless, this later visual strategy was a generative system, one in which he could use rules to create many "words." His earlier visual design strategy, in contrast, was not generative. It was a static, visual re-creation system, one that required each word to be seen and then learned, a system that would have served him well had he been learning to write Chinese instead of English. Of course, at this early date, Adam hadn't seen enough words to generate any generalizations or rules. He had seen several different words, mostly his name and the names of the other children who attended his family day-care center. What he had noticed first was that each child's name had a unique design associated with that particular child. He hadn't yet noticed that similarities also existed amidst these differences.

Before he would get to his generative visual strategy, however, another thought apparently occurred to him: The oral version of his name and other words might be related to their written forms. This is the idea that followed his totally arbitrary visual re-creation notion. Now, he began to code beats, or syllables, he heard in his name and other words with one mark each (e.g., AO for A-dam).

These three early hypotheses about how words are created—physical resemblance, visual re-creation, and syllabic representation—are described in this chapter. Later chapters include a discussion of only one or two hypotheses. Adam's first three hypotheses are covered in a single chapter because they emerged over a remarkably brief period of time, a span of just two and a half months. In contrast, Adam used some of his later hypotheses for as long as a year.

Figure 1–1

Notes   Adam did the drawing in Figure 1–1 while he sat at the kitchen table. He drew what looked like a human face, and underneath added what I thought was an approximation of the letters used to write his name. I looked at the paper and asked him to "tell me about this." While gesturing toward the picture, he said it was "a boy." Then he pointed to the three lines underneath the picture and said, "These are three two's for Adam." I was puzzled, because

he hadn't explained the first mark, which looked to me like an approximation of the letter A. "What's this mark?" I asked, as I pointed to it.

"Nothing," he replied.

"And what are these?" I asked, as I ran my finger under the three vertical lines.

"Three two's for Adam," he answered once again. "I two."

"That's your name?" I queried further.

"Yes."

Quickly, I wrote his name out in its standard form on another piece of paper. "But I thought this was what said Adam," I told him, as I showed him what I had written.

"No," he replied. "That has four; I two."

Comments   This was the first time that Adam had used marks to make a word. I didn't think to ask him at the time if the "writing" was a label for the picture (if the picture was Adam) or if it was a signature, indicating who had made or owned the picture. In any event, though its function remains a mystery, this was the first word Adam created.

At first glance, I assumed that Adam had made four marks, one each for the four letters used to write his name. But he hadn't. Perhaps he had started to make an A, which he had

Figure 1–1   Adam's Name
(Age 2 Years, 8 Months)

seen many times at the beginning of what people referred to as his name, but then disregarded it, thinking that the use of a certain number of marks, rather than marks formed in a specific way, was the primary consideration one needed to attend to when creating words. This hypothesis about words maintained that a physical relationship existed between the object itself and the word that stood for it. For a person, Adam thought the relationship should capture the quality of age, which he indicated by trying to equate marks with years lived. Apparently, he got carried away with his line making and made three, one more than necessary, to represent his two years.

When I presented his name, written in conventional form, he stated clearly why he rejected it: "That has four; I two." I've since been puzzled about why he disregarded his first marking, which approximated an *A*, and went on to create three vertical lines. I've often wished that I had written his name again, using just an *A* and a *D*, to see if he would have accepted this way of retaining a relationship between written marks and age. Perhaps he wouldn't have. Perhaps he used vertical marks to represent his name because he was accustomed to raising two fingers to answer the query "How old are you?" If this

was his reasoning, then there were two ways that he maintained a physical ralationship between himself and the symbols he used to represent himself: He captured the quantitative quality of his age, and he captured the actual physical resemblance of his fingers, when he used them to tell someone how old he was.

Even though this sample contained Adam's first instance of name writing, writing was not yet for him the abstract system that it is for us. It was still very much a picture of reality, in that it retained some physical relationship to what it was intended to represent. Nevertheless, it differed from pictures in one way: in its organization on the page. The vertical lines were arranged linearly, not scattered about in a more picturelike design. Adam did not yet understand what writing was, but he was beginning to know how it was supposed to look.

Figure 1–2

Notes   One day Adam came into the kitchen where I was writing at the table. "How do you make an *A*?" he asked. As he climbed onto a chair at the table, I wrote a large uppercase *A* on a piece of paper and gave it

Figure 1−2   Adam's *A* (Age 2 Years, 9 Months)

assumed at the time that it was because this letter is in his name and that he was trying to figure out how to write that. But he had used vertical lines to represent his name just a month earlier, so I had no good reason, at this point, to believe that he was asking about *A*'s so that he could write his name. However, by this time he might have been giving up his earlier idea that words should resemble their referents physically. In fact, the only time he ever used the physical-resemblance strategy to write his name or anything else was the instance shown in Figure 1−1.

Figure 1−3

Figure 1−3   Adam's Name (Age 2 Years, 9 Months)

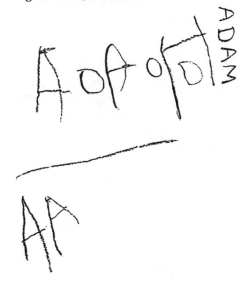

to him. He then took my pencil and his own piece of paper and copied my *A* (Figure 1−2). First he created an *A* positioned on its side (the upper middle portion of Figure 1−2). Then he made other marks, none of which turned out to look as much like an *A*.

Comments   This was the first time that Adam had asked me how to make an *A*. I wished later that I had asked him why he wanted to know how to make an *A*. I just

Notes   Adam created the writing sample in Figure 1−3 while in family day-care. It did not accompany a picture; it appeared by itself on a piece of paper. His day-care provider told me that other children had been writing their names on paintings and drawings. Adam, who hadn't been painting or drawing at the time, asked for a piece of paper on which to write his name. Figure 1−3 is what he created. (The name in the upper right corner was placed there by his caregiver after Adam had written his name.)

Comments It was fourteen days—exactly two weeks—between the time that Adam asked me to show him how to make an *A* and the time he created the sample shown in Figure 1–3. In the intervening two weeks, I am not aware of a single instance when he attempted to write his name, although he had brought home five or six paintings and drawings on which his day-care provider had written it. Then, all of a sudden, he tried to write his name himself.

This attempt, which differed from his first, suggested that he had changed his hypothesis about the way words are generated. No longer did Adam seem to think that a word should capture some physical characteristic of the object represented. In fact, he seemed to have accepted the arbitrary nature of words. He seemed to have said to himself, "You keep saying that this design says 'Adam.' Okay, I'll accept that and try to figure out how to write it myself."

The *A*'s were upright, not lying on their sides the way he had made them in his earlier attempt. And there was an *O*, which he would use for a very long time to placehold the *D* in his name. Next was a second *A*, followed by a small *O* and what looked like a goalpost with a circle under it.

I've always wondered about the small *O* after the second *A*. Was it used at first to placehold *M*, which Adam thought too hard to make? Did he then go on to attempt to make an *M*? Because he could not make the diagonal lines that belong at the top of an uppercase *M*, did he use the circle placed inside his "goalpost" in an effort to carve out some space around the goalpost to resemble the letter *M*?

I've wondered, too, about the meaning of the two *A*'s that appear below the line. Was he again thinking that because he was two he should use just two marks for his name? Or was he attempting to write all four characters in his name a second time and inadvertently made two *A*'s in succession?

The fact that Adam included a line on his paper between his two samples of writing suggests the extent to which he had begun to attend to the design aspects of writing, to how it should look. Often, at home, he wrote on lined sheets of white or yellow paper because this was the kind of paper I typically wrote on and gave him when he asked if he could have some. In fact, I often gave a pad to him when it was down to the last five to ten sheets, as a way to keep him away from my own. He may have thought writing was accompanied by lines. Given an unlined sheet of paper, he added the lines himself!

Figure 1—4

Notes   Adam created this drawing at his family day-care center. It was done on discarded computer paper, with crayon.

Comments   I noticed immediately that the circle and the *A* appearing above the large figure's head were green, while the other figures were either orange or red. I wondered if the green circle was also supposed to be a person but noticed that it lacked a mouth, which all of the other figures had. I assumed that the circle belonged with the *A* and that both together were intended to be Adam's name.

Given Adam's previous attempt to use more than two characters to write his name, I wondered why he had used just two here. Had he decided to use marks that looked like writing but still thought it important to retain some numerical correspondence between his name and his age? And what had happened

Figure 1—4   Syllables (Age 2 Years, 9 Months)

to his intervening idea that writing was arbitrary, not related physically to the objects it represents?

I doubt that Adam was reverting to the earlier notion that he needed just two marks to write his name because he was two. Instead, I think he was using another new hypothesis, one that said, "Oral and written language are related. Make one mark for every beat you hear in a word." Adam had begun to represent syllables.

Figure 1−5

Notes In the two samples in Figure 1−5, Adam used a syllabic hypothesis to write his name.

I asked Adam to tell me about the picture in Figure 1−5A. He pointed to the figure and said it was a boy. When I pointed to the letters in the upper-right-hand corner and asked him to tell me about them, he said, "A−dam S." He pointed to one letter as he said each syllable. He called the drawing in Figure 1−5B a boy as well and said that the two letters, *A* and *O* (reading right to left), said, "A−dam." He again pointed to one letter as he pronounced each syllable.

Figure 1−5 Syllables. A: Age 2 Years, 10 Months. B: Age 2 Years, 10½ Months.

A

B

Comments In the two samples in Figure 1–5, Adam made it clear that he was indeed coding syllables when he wrote his name. Yet in Figure 1–5A, when he wrote *ADS* (right to left), it appears that he used only one letter, *S*, to code his entire last name, which contains three syllables. Actually, he didn't intend to represent his full last name. In his family day-care center, there was a second child named Adam. The caregiver referred to the two boys as "Adam S" and "Adam M," not "Adam Matthews" and "Adam Schickedanz." Sometimes, when asked what his name was, Adam would answer that it was "Adam S." (This is a good example of how a complete understanding of the child's life is necessary if a child's writing samples are to be accurately interpreted.)

Figure 1–6

Notes Adam created Figure 1–6A one day while I was writing letters to some relatives. Adam asked for some stationery, which I gave him. He wrote a row of *O*'s (no doubt *D*'s to him), and then a row of *A*'s above it. When I asked him to tell me about his paper, he read it, using a reading intonation, "Dear Mom, I love you."

Figure 1–6 Syllables. A: Age 2 Years, 10 Months. B: Age 2 Years, 10$\frac{1}{2}$ Months.

A

B

Figure 1—6B was created twenty-two days after Figure 1—6A. I had been working at the computer when Adam asked me for a piece of paper. He took the piece of white computer paper I gave him and made some marks. When finished, he showed it to me and told me it said, "Dear Mommy, How I love you." He pointed to one mark for each syllable he said, coordinating marks and syllables exactly.

Comments   Here again Adam coded oral language in terms of syllables. But unlike the examples in Figure 1—5, where *A* and *O* (meaning *D*) represent the first phonemes in the two syllables of Adam's name, the letters used in the messages shown in Figure 1—6 bear no phonetic relationship to the words Adam said he had written. For these, too, he used his familiar *A*'s and *O*'s. These samples make clear that Adam's correct use of *A* and *O* to represent the beginning sounds of the two syllables in his name was simply a result of his limited writing repertoire—these were the only letters he knew how to make—and not an indication that he knew any specific letter-sound associations. Although Adam was now using a sound-based system to generate words, it was not a phonemic-based system; nor did he have any knowledge of phonics. It was a syllabic system, one in which each beat of a word was recorded by one letter, which Adam simply pulled from the limited rep-

ertoire of letters he knew how to create.

Yet on several occasions during this period, it appeared that Adam wasn't writing his name using a syllabic system of coding. For example, on May 15, which fell between the time that he made the two samples shown in Figure 1—6A and B, Adam created several pictures and then wrote on his paper what I thought was his name. On one of these, he wrote this:

I didn't ask him about it, because I simply assumed that it was his name.

On another picture, he wrote this:

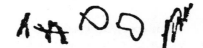

This time, I did ask him what he had written, because he had used five marks instead of four. When queried, he pointed to the first three marks as he said, "From A—dam." Then he paused, apparently because he was puzzled about the two remaining characters. He repeated the reading several times, with finger-pointing, until finally he read it like this: "From A—uh—d—um," which accounted for all five marks.

I suspect that he had intended only to code "From A—dam" but had gotten off track due to his knowledge about how his name usually looked. Perhaps he made the first mark to code "From," and then intended to write just two more—an *A* and an *O*—to code "A—dam." But instead, he wrote four characters, which is what he always saw others write when they made his name.

I wonder what caused Adam to begin to think about speech in terms of syllables. Perhaps it was caused by some songs he had learned from records played frequently at his family day-care center. His favorite, which he often sang when playing around the house, was "Baby Beluga." The rhythm of this song is very clear, and multisyllabic words are broken up nicely into syllables: "Ba-by Be-lu-ga in the deep blue sea. Swim so fast and swim so free. Hea-ven a-bove and the sea below, with a lit-tle white whale on the go. Ba-by Be-lu-ga. Ba-by Be-lu-ga . . ." Also, one of

Adam's favorite books at the time was *Dr. Seuss's ABC*, which I remember we always read very rhythmically:

Big A
Lit-tle a
What be-gins with A?
Aunt An-nie's All-i-ga-tor . . . A . . . a . . . A
Big B
Lit-tle b
What be-gins with B?
Bar-ber, ba-by, bub-bles, and a bum-ble-bee.

Perhaps it was these oral language experiences that caused Adam to begin to listen to and segment speech in terms of syllables. But this leaves unanswered where he got the idea that written language should represent oral language. I don't remember any instances of writing anything down for him and speaking out loud as I wrote. Even if I had, I wouldn't have coded the speech syllabically, though this doesn't necessarily mean that Adam wouldn't have done so himself, had he seen such demonstrations. It is entirely possible that some encounter with the word *Adam* on a note, perhaps from his grandmother, was pointed at and read to him, maybe even in "A—dam" fashion. Or, I might sometimes have run my finger under print as I read a story, although I don't remember doing this during this stage of his life.

Adam's use of the syllabic hypothesis was short-lived, spanning only a six-week period. But even before it disappeared, there was a hint of what would replace it. In the sample shown in Figure 1–6B, we see that Adam varied the placement of the letters, with the result that no more than two of the same kind occurred in succession. He hadn't done this in his first syllabically coded message (Figure 1–6A). There he had placed all of one kind of mark in each of two rows. Later, when he created the second sample, Adam apparently was beginning to notice that marks within words must vary.

Adam might have continued to integrate his sound and visual knowledge about words, rather than abandoning the sound-based strategy entirely, had he written mostly messages. With a message composed of several words, none of which is separated from the others by space, the writing looks quite similar to the writing a child sees on book titles, storefronts, and road signs. Many messages, written syllabically, with words run together, compare in length to single words when they are written conventionally. But Adam's most frequent writing situation was one in which he wrote only his name on paintings or drawings. There, standing alone, the word he wrote didn't look much like the words he saw: It was too short. I think it was this discrepancy between his writing and the writing that he saw that made him give up his syllabic hypothesis altogether, in favor of a visually governed strategy, one that paid attention to specific characteristics, such as the number and variation of letters used.

"This Is How a Word Is Supposed to Look, but What Word Is It?"

Adam Discovers That Looking Like a Word Isn't All There Is to Being a Word

In this chapter, we see the writing that Adam produced when he was concerned about how writing should look. During this period, he generated words by following certain rules:

1. Words must contain multiple marks.

2. Words cannot contain too few or too many marks.

3. Marks within a word must vary, with no more than two of the same kind appearing in succession.

4. The same marks can be used to make different words, as long as their order is varied across the words.

When Adam first began to use this visual rule strategy, he assumed that every letter string was an actual word. To find out which word he had created, he would approach adults and ask, "What word is this?" Later, after several weeks of feedback, through which he often learned that the letters he had strung together did not yield a real word, his question changed. Now, he asked, "Is this a word?" "Is this one?"

Given the low probability for success with this approach, it is not surprising that Adam eventually gave it up. But at first his concept about word creation remained firmly en-

Figure 2−1   Fred's Piece (Age 3 Years, 6 Months)

trenched in the visual domain. Only his strategy changed. Instead of stringing letters together and asking if he'd made a word, he simply asked adults to spell words for him. This certainly must have seemed like a more efficient approach.

When Adam began to ask for spellings, the basis from which adults generated words could begin to be made explicit to him. When asked by a child to spell a word, many adults intuitively talk out loud in a searching sort of fashion, as if they have to think about how to spell the word the child has requested. When Adam asked me how to spell "Mommy," for example, I responded first by adopting a somewhat pensive look, and then said the word slowly, several times over, as if I needed to think about it. Then I vocalized each sound in turn, as I named the letters I selected, and recorded them. After a while (several weeks), I began to pause a bit longer, as if I were stumped. This gave Adam time to supply the name of the needed letter, if he knew it. I selected the places where I would pause, making sure they were spots where the letter selection was fairly easy.

This procedure gave Adam access to the phonemic basis of our writing system. It allowed him to observe it in a way that had not been possible previously. After a period of time, he abandoned his visual approach to word-making and substituted this new sound-based strategy, which allowed him to write words independently. He isolated phonemes he heard in words and coded them with specific letters. Not until he began to notice a discrepancy between his invented spellings and the spellings of others did he begin again to pay some attention to how words looked.

Figure 2−1

Notes   Adam wrote Figure 2−1 while at home. I asked him to tell me about it. "This is Fred's," he said. "It says, 'I love you.'"

Comments   Adam now had an imaginary playmate named Fred. I think we can assume that Fred's knowledge of writing mirrored that of his creator. And it's clear that Adam's knowledge at three and a half had increased a bit from a year earlier. The message in Figure 2−1 was not created using a syllabic hypothesis. There are far too many characters. This piece was not made to *sound* like writing; it was made to *look* like writing.

Remarkably, though Adam had never created them before, there seemed to be a *P* here, and also an *L* and an *E*. (He had drawn an *L* and an *E* about a year earlier, when he had tried to copy the forms of some of his magnetic letters.) Up until this point, the repertoire of letters that Adam knew how to make was limited to *A*, *O*, and a very crude *M*. Yet, within a few weeks of his having created Figure 2–1, Adam came home from day care with two inventory pieces, one referred to as "letters" (**Figure 2–2A**), and the other referred to as "numbers" (**Figure 2–2B**). With his new visual idea about how words should be generated, he seemed to be motivated to study letters carefully and to try to make some new ones.

Adam no doubt knew the order of the alphabet from a musical record. But his father and I weren't sure how he knew the graphic configuration of so many letters, although we knew he had seen all of the letters many times in his Dr. Seuss *ABC Book* as well as in his everyday world, where print appeared on everything, from food cartons to road signs. He also played with the magnetic letters on our refrigerator door, although the play had not been with writing. (He usually built train tracks with the letters.)

During this period, Adam also watched "Sesame Street" fairly consistently, sometimes twice a day. At the age of three years, two

Figure 2–2 Inventory Pieces. A: Letters. B: Numbers.

A

B

**Figure 2—3 List of Words
(Age 3 Years, 7 Months)**

months, he had begun to attend nursery school two days a week. There, he saw print on charts and signs and probably noticed the letters created by other children and teachers as they wrote names on paintings and drawings. When we thought about it, it seemed likely that Adam had had a great many opportunities to look at all of the letters of the alphabet, although we had never specifically tutored him on their names or their graphic forms, except in three instances when he had asked for help with *L*, *A*, and *M*. (Adam's extensive experience with drawing no doubt came in handy at this point. Controlling the formation of lines is the same skill in writing as it is in drawing. Once Adam was familiar with how letters looked, the task of creating them would not have created many mechanical problems, given his experience with drawing.)

Adam hadn't noticed the variety in the marks making up print until now. His pre-vious concepts of word-making hadn't required that he attend to this sort of variation. Now, with this latest concept, Adam was looking for and seeing something new in print. In very short order, he noticed, studied, copied, and mastered most of the uppercase alphabet letters.

Figure 2—3

Notes Adam wrote the list of "words" shown in Figure 2—3 on a piece of blue paper that he found in the writing center of his nursery school. I don't know if someone told him how to spell the word "Dada," which appears at the very top, or if the creation of this word was an accident. Adam then created other words by changing the order of the letters and adding three new ones (*E*, *T*, and *F*).

Comments Adam's teachers didn't remember if Adam told them anything about what his writing said or if he had asked them what words he had written. I also did not ask him questions about this piece of writing when he brought it home. Without knowing what the writing meant to Adam, we cannot be certain that this was a list of words or that they were generated by using visual rules. But it certainly looked like it was.

Figure 2−4

Notes The words shown in Figure 2−4 were made at home at about the same time that Figure 2−3 was created at school. I was working at my computer when Adam asked me for some paper to "do some work." I gave him some. First he created the words shown in Figure 2−4A. He brought the paper to me and asked, "What do these spell? What words are these?" I sounded them out. He laughed after I sounded out each one, apparently realizing that neither of these creations was a word, which I confirmed by telling him that they weren't "real" words. "They look like words," I explained, "but they're not."

He then went back to the spot on the floor where he had been writing and started to write on the second piece of paper. First he wrote "ADAJ" (Figure 2−4B). "What word is this?" he asked. Again, I sounded it out. Again, he realized that it wasn't a real word.

Figure 2−4 Words (Age 3 Years, 7 Months)

A

B

Figure 2—5   Valentine. A: The Envelope. B: Adam's Signature.

This special card
brings lots of love
And happy wishes, too,
That Valentine's Day
will really be
A happy day for you!

HOPE YOUR DAY
IS SPECIAL!

A   B

"I know a real word I can make," he announced, as he set off to do more writing. In a moment, he returned with the same piece of paper, showed it to me, and said, "This is a real word." He smiled broadly as I read the second word in Figure 2—4B.

"Yes," I said, "that's a real word. It says 'Adam,' doesn't it?"

Comments   In this episode, it was clear that Adam was trying to create words by using visual rules to guide his efforts. It also appears that he was using knowledge of known words. The first word in Figure 2—4A looks like a variation on the word "Mama." This word, as well as "Mommy," was one that he had seen once or twice, such as when his father had spelled it just a month earlier, when Adam wanted to write it on a valentine envelope (see **Figure 2—5A**).

The second word in Figure 2—4A appears to have been a variation of his name, which he often saw on the nursery school attendance and helpers charts, as well as under the hook in his cubby. He also signed his name on his paintings and on cards. (Figure 2—5B shows the signature he wrote in his valentine.)

I've always wondered about the circle Adam drew around the last three characters in the writing sample shown in Figure 2—4A.

I can only guess that his initial version of this word exceeded his rule about the maximum number of characters and that he attempted to reduce their number by grouping the last three together, making them appear to be one.

Adam's third attempt to create a word, the top line in Figure 2—4B, is also a variation on his name, this time one in which only the last letter is changed. Perhaps he thought that such a slight change was more likely to yield a real word. But it did not. Finally, in his fourth attempt (the bottom line of Figure 2—4B), he simply wrote a word that he knew: his name.

During this period, at the age of around three and a half, Adam did not often use paper for his word experiments. Instead, he generated words using the magnetic letters on our refrigerator door. It was at this point that Adam began to use these letters for writing-related purposes. Heretofore, they'd been used for construction and fantasy play. For example, he'd line them up to make trains, or train tracks, as mentioned earlier. Or he'd drop one or two to the kitchen floor, where they became fish in a lake.

Sometimes Adam appeared frustrated after he had made many "words," none of which turned out to be real ones. To reduce his frustration, I sometimes rearranged the letters, or added one or two, to make a real word. I didn't keep track of how often or how many times I intervened in this way, although I don't recall that I did very much of it. Adam usually started out wanting to make words himself. Only when he expressed disappointment in the results of his efforts did I intervene.

Sometimes I reminded him that he did know some words, including "Mom," "Mommy," "Daddy," and "Adam," usually by spelling these out myself when Adam wasn't there and then inviting him to look for them among the letters scattered about on the refrigerator. He enjoyed finding the words that I had hidden. Often, he would find them and then start to experiment with word-making of his own.

Figure 2–6

Notes   The words shown in Figure 2–6A were written one day when Adam spent the afternoon with me at Boston University. He wanted to see a room where I taught my classes. When we entered the room, he saw

Figure 2–6   Adam's Words. A: In the Classroom (Age 3 Years, 8 Months). B: At Home (Age 3 Years, 9 Months).

A

B

the chalkboard. Immediately, he said he wanted me to write words on the chalkboard for him to copy. Before we could start, I had to get the necessary supplies from my office. Upon returning to the classroom, I agreed to write words for him, as long as he'd tell me which ones he wanted. He dictated several, including "cat," "bat," "rat," "Hawkman," "tiger," "dragon," and "picture."

The words shown in Figure 2–6B were created about a month later, at home. Adam announced that he wanted to play school the way we had played it at Boston University. I explained that we had no chalkboard on which I could write words for him. "That's okay," he replied. "Just tell me the letters." We sat in the living room to play school, and I told him to tell me which words he wanted. As he named each word, I called out the letters needed to spell them. After I had dictated the letters for "cat," and he had written them down, he said, "Wait. I'm going to write 'cat' again." He did, apparently without referring to his earlier version. In his new version, he used *k*, not *c*, for the first letter.

Comments These two episodes marked a shift in Adam's word-creation strategies. Now he asked for spellings. Although his basic assumptions about how words are created had not changed (he still assumed that they were formed by following visual rules), his strategy

for learning words was different. Instead of stringing letters together and asking which word he had created or if he had created a real one, he was relying on an authority to supply him with actual words that he could learn.

In these episodes, Adam's goal seemed to be to study words and how they are made. His writing served no communicative function—he wasn't writing a message to anyone. He seemed simply to want to learn how words were spelled.

The words he requested often rhymed. For example, he dictated "cat," "bat," and "rat"; "cat," "flat," and "bat"; and "dog" and "log." This generation of rhyming words indicated that he was beginning to focus consciously on phonemes in words. His one instance of invented spelling, when he rewrote "cat" with a *k*, also confirmed that he was beginning to think about speech at the phonemic level and had begun to think about the sounds that some letters represent. Yet it would be a very long time, another year, before Adam would use this information to generate several words; and longer still—almost two years—before he would routinely generate words on his own, using his phonemic awareness coupled with extensive knowledge about letter-sound associations.

I suppose there will be those who argue that my willingness to spell words for Adam impeded his growth toward independent (though unconventional) spelling. I doubt it. I suspect that Adam—and other children—require considerable knowledge about phonemic segmentation and letter-sound correspondences before they can take off on their own to create spellings. I also suspect that they acquire this information in the form of fine-tuned tutoring, supplied by adults as they provide spellings children request, in a way that makes the basis for their letter selection explicit.

It is misleading, however, to suggest that Adam concentrated for a year on consolidating this information. In fact, there were long stretches of time between the ages of four and five when he wrote relatively little or (when he did write) concentrated on something other than how specific words are made. Sometimes he experimented with the arrangement of writing on a page. Several examples of this sort of experimentation are shown in **Figure 2-7**.

Furthermore, writing certainly was not Adam's only interest. At nursery school, he enjoyed active play at the block, water table, and dramatic play centers. His interests at home revolved around construction materials, including LEGO® building sets; drawing; and

Figure 2-7 Experimentation

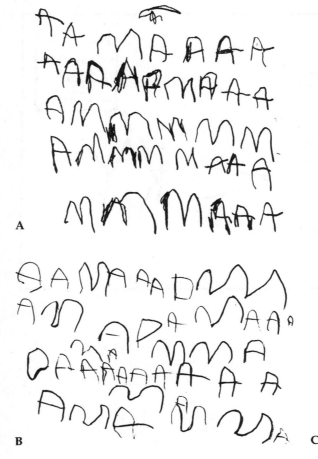

A

B

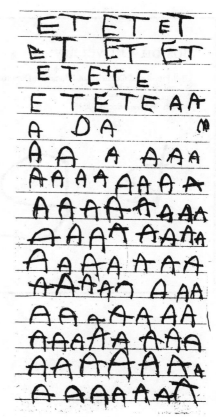

C

Figure 2—8   Envelope (Age 4 Years, 9 Months)

making things with paper, string, and tape. He spent hours on these activities, and often ignored his pencils and markers.

He also showed great interest in books during this period. He liked best books about dinosaurs, night and day, stars and planets, rockets and space exploration, the human body, and machines. He also enjoyed long stories and chapter books.

When Adam wanted to write words, he continued to ask for spellings or copied words from some environmental source (toys, books, signs, food cartons). For example, in **Figure 2—8**, we see an envelope that he addressed to a nursery school teacher when he was four years, nine months old. He copied her name from a name card located in the classroom writing center. A note that Adam wrote to me is shown in **Figure 2—9**. He was four years, eleven months at the time. He asked for the spelling of the word "love." He already knew the words "Mom" and "I." He generated the spelling of "you" ("U").

Eventually, independent phonemic-based spelling, whose beginnings we first saw when Adam was three years, nine months old (Figure 2—6B), overtook the other strategies entirely, enabling Adam to spell everything on his own.

Figure 2—9   Note (Age 4 Years, 11 Months)

"Mom, How Do You Spell /ch/?"

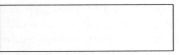

Adam Begins to Think About How Words Sound and to Forget About How Words Are Supposed to Look

As we have seen, flashes of insight about phonemic-based spelling and letter-sound correspondences apparently hit Adam from time to time before he settled firmly into using this strategy to create words. At first, Adam returned to more familiar strategies, much as an infant does when first learning to walk. In the beginning, the infant does not totally replace crawling with what we consider to be a more efficient way of getting around. Newly upright infants often drop to all fours, especially when they want to get someplace fast. It's only later, once they've really mastered walking, that their new mode of getting about seems to be easier than their earlier strategy of crawling.

In this chapter, we see Adam making more starts and stops, and then, finally, set out on a spurt of independent, phonemic-based writing. This was Adam's honeymoon with writing, the time when he thought it was easy.

Figure 3—1

Notes The writing shown in Figure 3—1 was a grocery list that Adam made for his father, who forgot, one day, to bring home items that Adam had requested. Because

**Figure 3–1 Grocery List
(Age 4 Years, 8 Months)**

Adam was disappointed about his father's memory lapse, I suggested that in the future he write down what he wanted his father to get.

Adam went immediately to the telephone, where a small pad of square paper is kept, and began to write the words "peanuts" and "cheese crackers," the items his father had forgotten. Adam wrote the *P* and the *E* for the word "peanuts" before pausing to ask me, "What comes after the *E*?" Then he asked what comes next, to which I answered, "An *N*." Then he added the *T* and *S* by himself.

Next, he began to write the word "cheese," asking me before he began how to write the /ch/ sound. (He made the sound and asked, "How do you write it?") He then added the *E* and the final *S* by himself.

Then he started to write the word "crackers." He wrote the first three letters—*C*, *R*, *A*—all by himself. Then he paused to ask if *C* or *K* is used. I told him that this word actually had both in its middle, with *C* coming first. He wrote these letters. Then he added the *R* and *S* by himself.

Comments This spurt of independent phonemic-based spelling appeared out of the blue. Except for the time that Adam had written the word "cat" ("KAT") some two months earlier, he had made no other attempts that I know of to spell words by isolating their sound segments and representing these with carefully selected letters of the alphabet.

But this latest attempt, like most of his early phonemic-based writing, was not done completely independently. He often asked for help. However, it is important to note that his requests for spelling information, at this point, almost always pinpointed specific sounds. He no longer asked for whole words, which was what he had done when asking for spellings during the latter part of his visual rule phase.

It would be another six months before Adam would compose complete messages using his newly acquired ability to isolate specific sounds in words and to select specific letters to represent the sounds he heard. In the intervening months, he used a variety of strategies. Sometimes he asked for spellings of words, sometimes he asked for spellings of sounds within words, sometimes he copied words, and sometimes he wrote words that he knew by sight. **Figure 3–2** provides a good example of a writing sample created by using a variety of strategies. The message was written when Adam was exactly five years old. It was written on two small cards that Adam found in his nursery school writing center one Saturday afternoon when the two of us went there to take care of the animals.

The message was for his former teacher. Adam asked me to spell "love," "you," and "dear." He also asked for the spelling of the middle sound in the word "miss." He knew his former teacher's name by sight even though he did omit (by mistake, I think) a *G* that comes before the *I*. He represented for himself the first and last phonemes in the word "miss," and omitted one of the *S*'s at the end.

Figure 3–3

Notes   Adam created the writing shown in Figure 3–3A at home. It was written on an odd-shaped piece of paper that he had found. He spelled all of the words completely independently and then gave it to me as a gift.

Adam also created the message in Figure 3–3B ("I love you") at home. He wrote it independently as well.

The writing shown in Figure 3–3C was also created at home. He wrote it while sitting on the sofa with his Cabbage Patch doll. I heard Adam say, "No, tiger, noses." When I glanced into the living room, I saw Adam writing something on a small pad of paper. When I asked him what he was doing, he said, "I'm teaching Terry [his doll's name] how to spell."

Figure 3–2   A Message (Age 5 Years)

Comments These samples constituted Adam's first real spurt of independent phonemic-based writing. They were created during the fall of Adam's kindergarten year. The first was created in September, the second and third in November.

Figure 3−3 **Writing at Home. A: A Gift (Age 5 Years, 2 Months). B: "I Love You" (Age 5 Years, 4 Months). C: "No, Tiger, Noses" (Age 5 Years, 4 Months).**

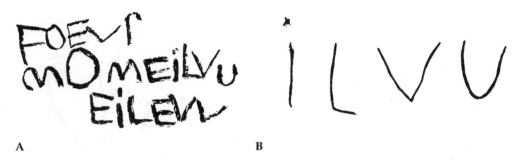

A

B

C

Figure 3−4

Notes Adam's kindergarten was very similar to his nursery school—very experience- and play-based, with no worksheets or reading readiness drills. However, the children were asked to do one activity weekly that did involve drawing, reading, and writing. This activity was a "Family Schoolwork" assignment (Figure 3−4). These assignments were sent home on Fridays and were due back the following Tuesday or Wednesday.

The kindergarten teachers always wrote explanatory notes on the schoolwork sheets. All during the fall, sheets bore a note that said, "Write the words yourself or ask your parent to write them for you." We always said to Adam, after discussing what would be put down, "Okay, write that on here." Then, if he said he didn't want to or that he wanted us to help him, we cheerfully pitched in.

Figure 3—4 Family Schoolwork. A: Age 5 Years, 2 Months. B: Age 5 Years, 4 Months. C: Age 5 Years, 4 Months.

FAMILY SCHOOL WORK--Bring this back to school on Mon., Tues., or Wed.

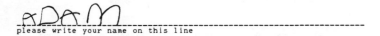

please write your name on this line

    This Family School Work is about bringing papers home from school and bringing them back to school again.

    With your parents, choose a place in your house where you will put your Family School Work each week when you bring it home from school.

    The place I will put my Family School Work each week is:

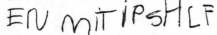

           (On my top shelf.)

(Write the words yourself or ask your parent to write them for you. On the attached paper, draw a picture of your Family School Work.)

A

FAMILY SCHOOL WORK

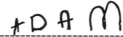

Write your name on this line or ask your parent to write it for you.

    Shapes are all around us. The shapes we've been talking about in school are: circle ○ , triangle △ , square ▢ , and rectangle ▭ .

    For your Family School Work this week, please take a "SHAPE WALK" inside or outside your house with your parent. Look for things that have circle, triangle, square and rectangle shapes. When you see something that has one of these shapes, tell your parent and he or she will write it down in that shape's space on the attached piece of paper. Try to find 3 things for each shape.

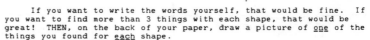

    If you want to write the words yourself, that would be fine. If you want to find more than 3 things with each shape, that would be great! THEN, on the back of your paper, draw a picture of <u>one</u> of the things you found for <u>each</u> shape.

NOTE TO PARENTS - Some approaches to doing this work are:
1. Ask your child which shape she'd like to do first, find 3 things with that shape and then choose another.
2. Look at an object and ask your child what shapes she sees in that object. Then choose other objects.
3. Think about some or all of the shapes as you walk and ask your child if he sees any of them.
4. If it doesn't seem challenging enough, use a timer and see how many shapes he can find in 10 seconds.

The approach you choose will depend on the learning style of your child. If your child has difficulty with one approach, try another.

B   *continued*

Figure 3-4 Continued

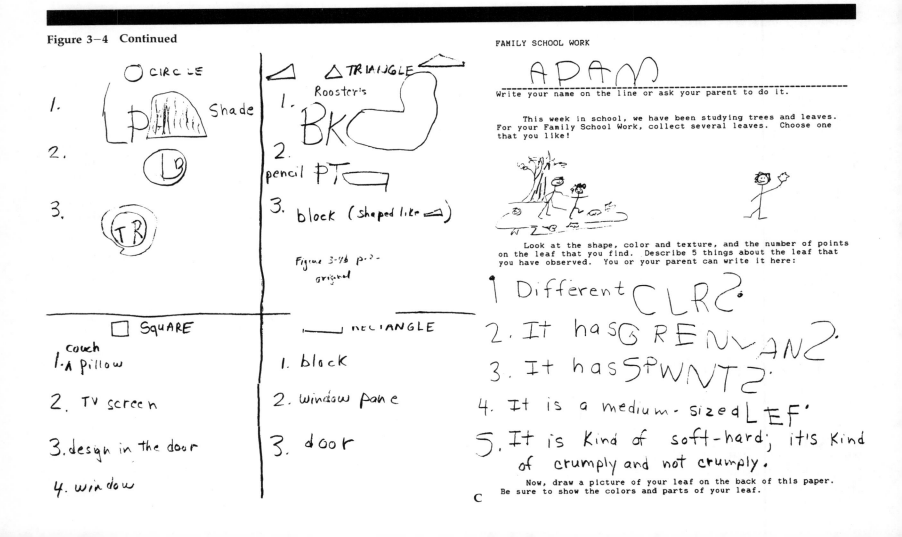

○ CIRCLE

1. Shade

2.

3. (TR)

△ TRIANGLE

1. Rooster's
    BK

2. pencil PT

3. block (shaped like ◁)

Figure 3-4b p.3-
original

□ SQUARE

couch
1. A pillow

2. TV screen

3. design in the door

4. window

▭ RECTANGLE

1. block

2. window pane

3. door

FAMILY SCHOOL WORK

A P A M

Write your name on the line or ask your parent to do it.

This week in school, we have been studying trees and leaves.
For your Family School Work, collect several leaves. Choose one
that you like!

Look at the shape, color and texture, and the number of points
on the leaf that you find. Describe 5 things about the leaf that
you have observed. You or your parent can write it here:

1 Different CLRS.

2. It has GREN VANS.

3. It has SPWNTS.

4. It is a medium-sized LEF.

5. It is kind of soft-hard; it's kind
   of crumply and not crumply.

Now, draw a picture of your leaf on the back of this paper.
Be sure to show the colors and parts of your leaf.

C

Comments It is obvious from the samples shown in Figure 3–4 that Adam used a phonemic-based system to generate words. It is also obvious that he often asked us to write down what he said instead of doing all of the writing himself. When we wrote down what he dictated, we generated the spellings ourselves instead of asking him to tell us how to spell the words. As far as we can recall, Adam remained quite attentive throughout these sessions and probably watched as we wrote down what he dictated.

Figure 3–5

Notes I helped out in the kindergarten on the day that Adam created the sample shown in Figure 3–5A. Children who were interested could make holiday-related stationery as a gift for their parents. Most children, however, decided to make greeting cards. Adam asked how to spell the words "Merry" and "Christmas," but spelled "Dad" all on his own.

A few days later, while at home, Adam used this card as a model to write another Christmas message to his dad, although he also generated other words ("I," "wish," "have") on his own (Figure 3–5B).

Figure 3–5 Christmas Messages (Age 5 Years, 5 Months). A: At School. B: At Home.

A

continued

Figure 3–5   Continued

B

A few days later he noticed the picture of his camp group from the previous summer, sitting on a shelf in the living room. He said that he wanted to write a letter to the Bullfrogs (his group's name). When writing this message, he asked me to spell every word.

Comments   The examples in Figure 3–5 illustrate that Adam's independent use of phonemic-based spelling emerged over quite a long period of time. At first he mixed it

with other strategies to create a piece of writing; then he'd use it independently for a while to create a whole piece himself; then he'd revert entirely to earlier strategies of asking for spellings or copying them. Sometimes, especially with the Family Schoolwork (Figure 3–4), where quite a lot of writing often had to be put down, he would generate a few words independently and then ask us to do the rest of the writing for him. It was not until the spring of his kindergarten year that he seemed truly to be launched on his independent phonemic-based writing spree.

Figure 3–6

Notes   Adam drew the picture of a bus shown in Figure 3–6 while he was at home one day. He labeled some of the bus's parts: window (WDO), Front window (Fit WDO), Door (DEr), Tire (Tir). He generated the spellings all by himself.

Comments   With the creation of this piece, done in late January, when he was just over five and a half years old, Adam began a four-month stretch of independent writing. During this period, he generated words by coding sounds he heard as he said the words. While he wrote, he sounded out the words, often bit by bit, while he recorded what he heard. At this point, he knew enough letter-sound associations to record most of the sounds he wanted to represent. Only occasionally did he ask how to spell a sound.

Sometimes, if he asked for the spelling of a short vowel, I would ask, "What word are you trying to make?" (I couldn't tell, for example, if he wanted to spell the vowel in the word "but" or the vowel in the second syllable of a word such as "Jonah.") He would let me know right away in these situations that he did not want me to spell the word: "I don't want you to spell the *word*; I just need to know how to spell this *sound*!" His view of the spelling system was so simple, at this point, that he was unaware of the ambiguity I was attempting to sort out. In such situations I began to peek over his shoulder to try to guess the word he was attempting to make so that I could decide what information to give. At the time, this approach seemed preferable to trying to explain the ambiguities of the spelling system. My primary goal at this point was to support Adam's independence. He thought he knew enough to write on his own, with just a little help, now and then, on

Figure 3-6   A Bus (Age 5 Years, $6\frac{1}{2}$ Months)

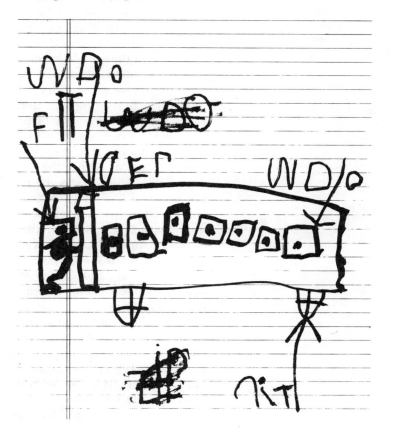

specific sounds. I didn't want to undercut his confidence by providing information that might make him feel that the task was beyond him, especially because he had done some independent spelling on several previous occasions and then had abandoned it for months at a time while he reverted to earlier, more dependent, strategies.

Later, I would wonder if I had done the right thing in making him think spelling was easier than it is. When he began to notice that his spellings did not look like the words he saw in books and the environment, he thought for a while that he just wasn't sounding out the words the right way. It did not occur to him that his assumptions about how spelling worked could be wrong, that not all words are perfectly phonetic. Looking back, I think I could have preserved his confidence in his ability to generate words without leading him so far astray about the realities of the spelling system by responding to his questions with a statement something like this: "I'm not sure exactly which letter you should use for that sound; in some words, we need to use an *A*, but in others, we need to use a *U*. Tell me the word you are trying to make, and then I can decide whether you need to write an *A* or a *U*." But, at the time, I didn't foresee the problem he would have

later, and I didn't know that the exact way in which I gave him help with his spelling would turn out to be so important.

Figure 3−7

Notes   The sample in Figure 3−7A was created at home, on a strip of paper. Adam wrote this as a valentine for his grandparents. It says, "For a best grandpa and grandma." Adam wrote all of it without asking for any help.

Figures 3−7B and 3−7C were small valentines for me and his dad. Figure 3−7D was another valentine that Adam made for his dad. He found a preprinted valentine and decided to add to it by attaching a piece of paper. He wrote an additional message on the paper: "Have a good Valentine's. Love, Adam."

Figure 3−7E was also a valentine. Adam cut and taped paper to make an alien, on which he then wrote the following message: "Be a good alien. I love you. Love, Adam."

Figure 3−7F shows all of the names he wrote on the valentines he sent to children and teachers in his kindergarten classroom. (I traced the names before he gave the valentines away.) The names in the columns

Figure 3—7 Valentines (Age 5 Years, 7 Months). A: To His Grandparents. B: To His Mother. C—D: To His Father. E: Another Valentine. F: Names of Those to Whom Valentines Were Sent in School.

(top to bottom, left to right) are: (column 1) Ethan, Matthew G., Matthew C., Wendel, Amanda; (column 2) Keisha, Ada, Hannah, Kate; (column 3) Robert, Miss Doane, Miss Danielson. The only time Adam asked for help was when he was writing the name Danielson. After he wrote up to the first *N*, he asked, "What comes next?"

Comments   Valentine's Day offered many opportunities for Adam to write. I purchased a bag of small valentines for him to give to classmates, but in addition to writing these, Adam spontaneously created others for family members. This was just one example of his interest in writing during this period. He truly seemed to enjoy it.

Adam's rendering of the word "love" on the alien card is interesting, given that here he included an *i* in the middle, whereas he wrote "love" with just an *L* and *V* on the other cards he made for me and his father. I don't know what prompted him to spell it "liv," but I suspect that instead of hearing a sound that he thought he would represent, he added the vowel just because it made the word look more like a word. I also suspect that he paused to ask me what came after the first *N* in the name Danielson for the same

reason. He had seen this word quite often, which meant that he had some specific visual knowledge about it. In these two cases, visual knowledge interacted with sound-based knowledge.

While Adam's writing during this phase was typified by the coding of sounds he heard, there were hints, such as the ones just mentioned, that he occasionally thought about how a word should look and modified the spelling accordingly. Later the discrepancy between how Adam's words looked when he coded sounds he heard, and the way he thought they should look from the way he had seen them, threw him for a cognitive loop. But before this inconsistency created a major stumbling block, Adam wrote a lot, sticking mostly to strict coding of sounds heard, with an occasional sight word thrown in.

Figure 3–8

Notes   Adam created Figure 3–8A one day when he was home from school with a strep throat. He had watched a program about snake charmers on the educational television channel. When it was over, he announced that he was going to draw a picture of a snake

Figure 3—8   At Home (Age 5 Years, 7 Months to 5 Years, 8 Months). A: "Snake Charmer." B: "Where Is the Lost Ark?" C: Numbers and Birthday List. D: Reporter.

charmer to give to his teacher the next day. He wrote the words "snake charmer" ("SNAKCHRMR") under the picture he drew. He drew and wrote all on his own.

Figure 3–8B was also created at home. Adam was playing reporter, which was a carryover from a time eight months earlier when he had played reporter in his nursery school's newspaper office. On this particular day, he used a small white note pad and a pencil. He came up to me and asked, "Mom, where is the lost ark?" I said, "I don't know, Adam; I don't know." Adam wrote this down, and then apparently added "yes" ("YIS") as a contrast to the word "know," which he spelled *NO*.

Figure 3–8C was also created at home. Its creation was prompted by a hand-held calculator, which I was using to work on our income tax return. Adam saw the calculator and asked to use it. I told him that he couldn't, because I needed to do my work. I told him that there were numbers on the typewriter and suggested that he might like to create some numbers using it.

He took my suggestion and put paper in the electric typewriter. Then he looked for the numeral 1 on the top row of typewriter keys. When he couldn't find it, he said, "There's not a one on this typewriter." I explained that the L key is used to type the numeral one, but this apparently made no sense to him, so

he just started typing numerals, beginning with 2. When he reached 10, he ran into difficulty again, because he couldn't find a 10. I tried to explain, once again, that he could use the L key, plus 0, to create a 10. But, because he couldn't understand how this could be done, he took the paper out of the typewriter and wrote 1, 10, 11, and 12 by hand.

When finished with this, he asked again for a turn with the calculator. I again said that he couldn't have a turn right then, because I needed to use it. Then he began to draw pictures on his paper. When he finished the pictures, he showed the paper to me and announced that these were the things he wanted for his birthday. Then he named them: "Calculator, Inhumanoid, Voltron, spaceship, backpack pack, teddy bear, Whiteout" (another of my possessions that he coveted). I responded by saying that his birthday was quite a while away—not until July—and that I wasn't sure that I could remember the names of all of the items, given that it was only March. (I had in mind the Voltron and the Inhumanoid, which I wanted to forget about!) "I'll write their names," he said, as he took hold of the paper. Away he went to do just that. When finished, he delivered the paper to me: "Here," he said. "I wrote their names so you won't forget what they are."

The writing shown in Figure 3–8D was created while Adam was playing reporter. This time, he used a very small pad of white notepaper and stood at the dining-room table, looking out the window. "I'm a reporter, and I'm writing down everything I see," he said. Some of the things he saw included cars ("KRS"), gates ("GATS"), trees ("TRES"), soil over the road ("SOIL OVR THEO RAD"), lamp-posts ("LAPOST"), signs ("SINS"), houses ("HAWSIS"), snow ("SNO"), and people bicycling ("PEPIL BICOEN").

Comments   In these samples, we see again the extent to which Adam was writing independently. We see, as well, a tendency for him to add soft vowels. He almost always represented the short *A* sound, no doubt because it is contained in his name. But he also included some short *I*'s: two in the word "Inhumanoid," another in the word "soil," one in the second syllable of the word "people," and one each in the words "spaceship," "teddy," "bear," and "houses." I think these additions were now guided by sound, not by sight. When Adam said the words before writing them, he exaggerated the sounds, including vowels, that they contained.

These samples also illustrate the situations that prompted Adam to write. In one case, he was out of school because he was sick. I think he wanted some way to link back up with his teacher the next day when he returned. He decided his bridge back to school would be a picture. It was not unusual for me and for other parents to drop notes off with the teacher when we dropped off our children at school. As a result, Adam was accustomed to the idea that a note written at home could be delivered to the teacher.

Two of the samples in Figure 3–8 were created during pretend play, with a theme Adam had first been introduced to several months earlier, at nursery school. Because writing was required to enact the role of reporter, which he always chose to play, the play prompted him to do some writing.

One sample, Figure 3–8C, was prompted by an observation of me. I was using a calculator, and he wanted a turn. In this case, writing was used to get a message across and to aid my memory. Adam had seen these functions of writing modeled at home many, many times. We always use a grocery list for shopping, for example. In fact, a piece of paper is always posted on the refrigerator door, making it easy for someone to jot down the name of a needed item.

Figure 3–9   Dragon Book (Excerpts) (Age 5 Years, 7 Months)

All of the writing episodes out of which the samples in Figure 3–8 were produced were prompted by Adam's social knowledge, by situations in which he had observed adults write. Although on these four occasions Adam seemed spontaneously to come up with the idea that he would write, that writing was an option at all was because of his particular social history. It didn't just unfold from within him, without the help of any external factors.

Figures 3–9, 3–10, 3–11

Notes   The samples shown in Figures 3–9 and 3–10 were written at school. Figure 3–9 was written in February, during a week or two when the children learned about the Chinese New Year (thus, the dragon). Figure 3–10 was written in late March or early April. All during the year, the children learned about various animals. I'm not sure if children were told to write stories about animals in blank books, which were available, or if the topics were open-ended and Adam chose to write his about cheetahs.

Figure 3-10 Cheetah Book (Excerpts) (Age 5 Years, 8 Months)

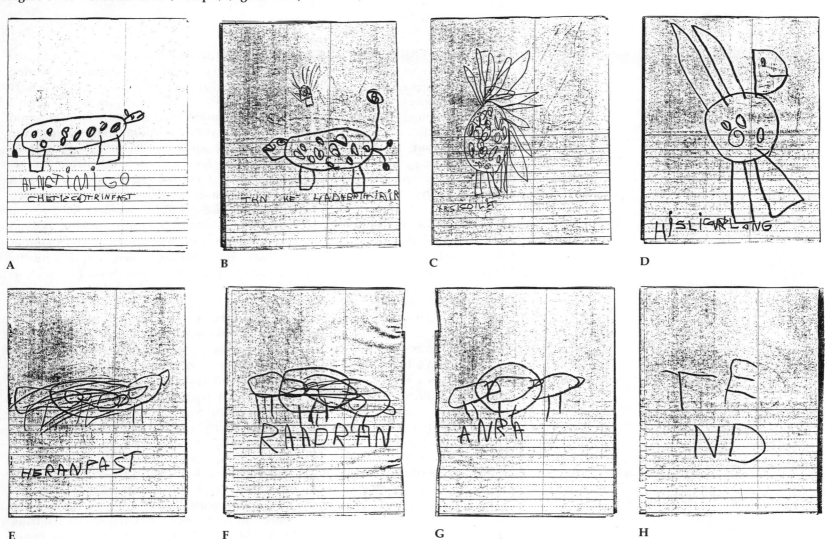

The book excerpted in Figure 3–11 was school-related but was written at home, as a Family Schoolwork assignment. As part of the children's study of animals, they learned about baby animals, including themselves. For Family Schoolwork, the children were to find out vital information about their birth, such as their birthdate and their birth weight and length. In addition, they were to ask their parents about some of the things they did when they were a baby. Then they were to draw a picture of themselves doing this thing, and to write a description if they wanted to. All of these pages were sewn inside a heavy posterboard cover, which became the child's Baby Book. Adam loved hearing about the things he did as a baby, and he wanted to draw pictures and write about each activity.

Comments   All of these books were created during what I call Adam's first independent writing phase. As far as I know, the books completed at school (Figures 3–9 and 3–10) were written completely without help. With the dragon book, his teacher apparently wrote in standard spelling above Adam's words, as he read the story to her, perhaps as an aid to his parents, who later would try to read it.

In his dragon story, as well as in the Baby Book, we see Adam's tendency during this time to use numerals to spell words (1 combined with an *S* to form the word "once"; 2 used consistently in the Baby Book to stand for the word "to"). Adam didn't stop using numerals to spell words until some months later, after he received a calculator for his birthday and got interested in writing down numerals and equations. (His kindergarten program wisely, I think, avoided dealing with math in symbolized form, stressing instead experiments with measurement and manipulatives, the results of which were left mostly unrecorded, except in rare instances such as the sheets about birth height and weight, which became part of the Baby Book.) Only in the early summer, after the kindergarten year had ended, did Adam really begin to grasp some number knowledge in a generative, relationship sort of way. At this point, he became interested in writing down his number knowledge. In one such episode of mathematical exploration, he asked me, while we rode in the car to a restaurant, to ask him some sums, which he dictated one at a time: $6 + 6$, $7 + 7$, $8 + 8$, and so on. He gave the answer to each problem I posed; to the sums just mentioned, he answered 12, 13, and 14. I asked him each time, "Are you sure?" "I'm sure," he responded, so I left it at that, realizing what his error was, but appreciating none-

Figure 3–11 Baby Book (Excerpts) (Age 5 Years, 9 Months)

My name is ADAMDAVO SCHICKEDANS

My birthday is JULYO

When I was born I weighed E L I V I N (eleven) Pounds 2 ounces

When I was born I was

22 inches long.

A

ILNTA K BSOF
TH SHLF A DL KATHM

B

ILVDABATH

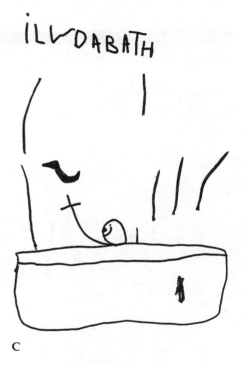

C

ILIDSPLNTH
TOYLITPAPR

D

Figure 3—12 Math Problems

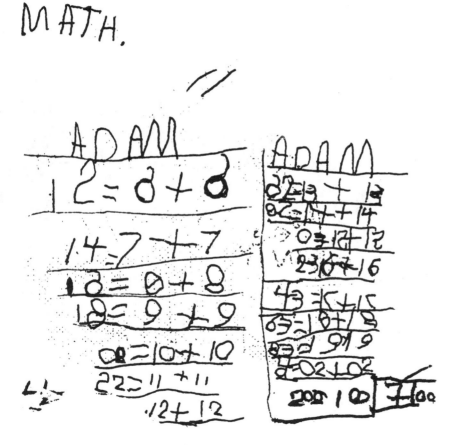

theless his interesting strategy (he was adding integers successively one more than the last one, but he was forgetting to account for both in figuring the sum).

When we arrived at the restaurant, he asked for a pen so that he could write down the "math problems" (his terminology) on a cocktail napkin he had found on the table. He wrote "math" at the top of the napkin, spelling it correctly, and then wrote his name, under which he drew a line. Then he began to record the sums he previously had calculated in his head while riding in the car (see **Figure 3—12**). Suddenly he said, "No, I wasn't sure! There are two, not one!" He had detected his earlier error.

Adam's sums, when written, were correct as far as the math was concerned, although each equation was written from right to left, not left to right, and most of the individual numerals were reversed. He appears to have miscalculated some of the sums, because he reversed the order of the numerals when he recorded two-digit numbers (e.g., 62 instead of 26 for 13 + 13; 82 instead of 28 for 14 + 14, etc.). There was a lot for Adam still to learn about how to write numerals. But the lesson he did learn from writing down his mathematical ideas was that numerals are not used to write words. They are used in other writing situations instead, those that we refer to as "doing math."

Numerals are used in other situations as well, which Adam began to notice. He had placed them on the picture of the calculator he drew in late March as part of the list of items he wanted for his birthday (Figure 3–8C). In mid-July, he did an inventory of situations in which numerals are used. As can be seen in **Figure 3–13**, he included his birthday (July 6), his telephone number (with many numerals still reversed), and a drawing of a calendar, which he did not know contains numerals only up to 31. (He also organized the numerals in columns instead of in rows and organized the rows themselves from right to left instead of from left to right.)

It was only after Adam had begun to write and draw about math that he stopped including numerals in the representations of sounds he heard in words. He had long ago figured out that numerals were to be used in writing rather than in picture-making, but it was only now, more than two years later, that he had figured out in exactly which contexts numerals were to be written down. (See Appendix B for a discussion of Adam's development in distinguishing writing from pictures.)

Figure 3–13   An Inventory

Figure 3–14

Notes One day, some weeks after Adam worked on his Baby Book at home, he stapled several blank pieces of typing paper together and brought them to me. "Let's make a book together. You write a page and then I'll write a page," he suggested. I agreed to participate in the joint project. Before we started to write, he said, "Now let's be considerate of each other, okay? Let's write from left to right." I agreed that this would be a good idea, so we wouldn't get "mixed up reading it." Adam titled the book "A Apple Eater," and we began (Figure 3–14).

Comments Several aspects of the writing shown in Figure 3–14 are worthy of note. First, with the exception of his Baby Book, which was prompted by a school assignment, Adam had never written a story at home. I think the idea occurred to him because he had been writing stories at school and because we had worked together on his Baby Book project.

Second, his effort to reach agreement with me concerning the direction in which we would write indicated the dawning of a new insight. In his earlier writing, he had not shown any particular awareness that writing must be placed on the page in just one direction. I don't know where he acquired this new awareness. Perhaps someone at school had mentioned it to him. In any event, his initial understanding did not seem to encompass the extent to which this convention applied within a given language. He seemed to think that writing could be oriented in any direction as long as it was consistent within a piece of writing and all involved parties agreed. He didn't realize that writers are not free to take such liberties.

His confusion on this point might have been due to the fact that several children in his kindergarten classroom spoke Hebrew and perhaps could write in Hebrew as well. I think his teachers often talked about different ways of doing things as a way to promote multicultural understanding and appreciation. Perhaps his teachers talked about the different ways writing in different languages can be arranged on a page; perhaps they commented that people can decide which of several ways they want to do things. Adam apparently understood his teacher to mean that this freedom applied to separate occasions within a language, instead of only across languages.

Figure 3-14   Jointly Written Book (Excerpts) (Age 4 Years, 9 Months)

THE APALETR wissiTENiORA APiLTRE.

Chp. 1

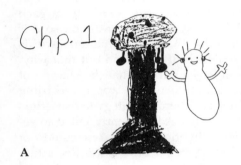

A

The apple eater decided to eat the apples.

B

THE APALETRBRT

C

Then, the apple eater decided to take a nap.

D

THE APALEYR WiGiTE NeMiRED GiT.

E

H EWGTdiNiMNiT

F

THAHAASiRiMONE

G

The third interesting aspect about this book-writing episode was that Adam didn't alter his spellings, even though I used many of the same words, spelled conventionally, when it was my turn to write a page. Although Adam always watched carefully as I wrote, he didn't seem to notice, or at least didn't comment about, the discrepancies.

Fourth, we can see a lot of what I call "recording errors," a failure to represent sounds actually heard. Adam had made such errors before—for example, in his Cheetah Book (Figure 3–10) he had left out the letter *N* at the end of the word "ran" and wrote "and" without the final *D* (Figure 3–10F, G). Other examples of recording errors can be seen in his Baby Book (Figure 3–11), where he left out the final *G* in the word "taking" (Figure 3–11B), the *V* in the word "loved" (Figure 3–11D), the *A* in the middle of the word "play" (Figure 3–11D), and the *O* in the word "go." This last error occurred in a sentence that reads, "I loved to go on the swings." The deletion of the *O* could have been in the word "on," not in the word "go." Perhaps Adam got confused about what he had written and thought the *O* he had recorded for the word "go" was the *O* he needed for the word "on." Another error of this kind also occurred on the page shown in Figure 3–11B. He had wanted to say, "I loved taking books off the shelf and looking at them." When he wrote the words "at" and "them," he made them share the *T*: "ATHM." Again, this probably was a recording error, although Adam might have thought that the same letter could be shared by two successive words. He had not yet begun to separate words from each other by leaving space between them, so it is possible that he thought contiguous words could share letters, if it worked out that way.

What makes me think that the sharing of letters between two words was a recording error and not a deliberate strategy to use letters efficiently was that Adam clearly failed to record letters in situations where one could not be "borrowed" from a nearby word. Recording errors abound in his Apple Eater book, and he detected these when he reread it. In fact, he became quite upset upon discovering that he "didn't write it right." At first he was sure he had ruined the book, because there was no room in the line to squeeze the missing letters in. Then I suggested that we fix it by writing the letters above or below the line of writing, close to where they had been left out. He liked this solution and wrote some corrections himself, although he asked me to do some of them.

Before this episode, I hadn't considered how difficult the task of recording actually is. I had conceptualized writing merely in terms of a child having to know a letter that could represent each sound heard in a word. But the organizational task really is much more complicated than this. I suspect that children, like adults, generate whole sentences (at least this much) when they are in the process of composing a story. I know that Adam did, because he always said a whole sentence before starting to write anything down. If a child generates words by coding each sound heard instead of by knowing automatically (as with sight words) the letters that are needed, the child has to say each sound, record it, say the next sound, record it, and so on, until the whole word is coded. But of course children typically need to say the whole word again to prompt themselves into remembering which sound they need to record next. And they are doing this while they are trying to remember which sound within the word is the last one they recorded. Then it's on to the next word of the story, which often must be remembered by restating the whole sentence. Then the child must check again to recall which word was last recorded, so as to be sure that he or she starts with the right word from the yet-to-be-recorded group.

All of this requires tremendous coordination between an oral message, which is stored in the child's head, and the message that is being written down. And all of this has to be done under the stress that is involved in not being quite sure of letter-sound correspondences—of having to think each one out. This takes time, which, in turn, results in a lot of interruption in the child's train of thought. It is no wonder that young children find writing to be such hard work and so tiring. Perhaps this is why Adam wanted us to take turns in writing the Apple Eater book.

Figure 3–15

Figure 3–15 "Cat"
(Age 5 Years, $9\frac{1}{2}$ Months)

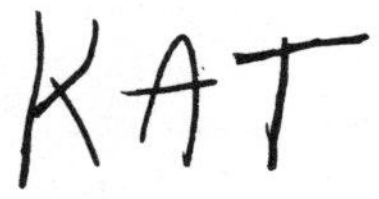

KAT

Notes At home one day near the end of April, Adam asked me how to spell the word "cat." He was holding a small pad of paper in his hand at the time, and I could see that he had already written "KAT" on it (Figure 3–15). I asked him how he thought "cat" should be spelled. "Well," he said, "I thought it was spelled with a *K*, because it sounds like a *K*. But I think I saw it someplace and it was spelled with a *C*."

I told Adam that he was right, that the word "cat" was spelled with a *C*, not a *K*. I went on to explain that *C* is a tricky letter, that it sometimes is used to represent the /s/ sound, and that other times it is used to stand for the /k/ sound.

"Oh," he said, as he went off. (He didn't change the way that he had written the word.)

Comments Although I didn't know it at the time, this event was a very important one for Adam. Whether this specific event triggered the beginning of Adam's awareness that his words did not look right, or whether Adam commented on a possible discrepancy between his version and other versions of the word "cat" because he'd already begun to notice such discrepancies, I do not know. I do know that he had looked several times at the Apple Eater book we had written together without any comment about the different ways that he and I had spelled various words. Or perhaps he had noticed, and this was the source of his new uncertainty about the words he generated by coding sounds. Or perhaps some peer at school had told him that his words were wrong. This might have caused him to scrutinize his words more closely. It is impossible now to know just when and why the questioning of Adam's own sound-based spellings began.

No matter when he had had the first inkling that his words looked different than words written by others, the idea had begun to affect his writing behavior by the beginning of June. By then, he rarely wrote anything at home. In addition, when he brought his last book of the year home from kindergarten in late June, I noticed at once that he hadn't written it by himself. (See **Figure 3–16**.) The first part of each page, except for the last one, was not written in Adam's handwriting. (A classmate's mother, who had been volunteering for the day, had written it for him, he told me.) And the last few lines on the pages, which were in his own handwriting, contained far more conventionally spelled words than was typical. "Ethan [a friend] helped me," he said.

"Why didn't you write your own book?" I asked. "You wrote all of your other books."

"Because I can't make the words *look* right," he replied.

"Oh, you are a good writer," I said, trying to be supportive.

"No, I'm not," he replied. "No matter how hard I try to sound them out, they still don't look right."

Adam would not write again for a very long time, not until he had to after he entered first grade the next September. And even in first grade he dreaded writing, even hated it, because he still couldn't make his words "look right," as he put it. He said several times during the spring, and then again in the fall, that no matter how hard he tried to sound the words out, he couldn't get them to look right. He was saying very explicitly what his stumbling block was: He thought that the only way to spell words was to sound them out and to code what you hear. But I didn't listen to what he was saying, or have the sense to tell him, "Oh, lots of words aren't spelled the way they sound. Some words have silent letters, double vowels, and all kinds of tricky spellings, which you can figure out by following some special rules and by learning how some words are spelled. Words don't look right if you just rely on sounding them out. Spelling is not that simple."

It would take a crisis of sorts in the fall to prod me into responding to Adam's problem. And even then I would discover by accident that it was a conceptual hurdle that I had to help him get over.

Figure 3–16   Adam's Last Book of the Year (Excerpt) (Age 5 Years, 11 Months)

"So, If You Didn't Know About Silent *e*, You'd Just Waste *k—i—t* When You Wanted to Spell *kite*. Right?"

Adam Learns Why Spelling Needs to Be Hard

In this chapter, we see Adam during a time when he thought writing didn't make sense, when he felt defeated by it. We see his dry spell at the age of six, when his cognitive confusion stopped the flow of words that previously had gone so easily from mind to hand. Then we see a prolific period of writing follow, as his conceptual stumbling block, the source of his writing crisis, was resolved. At the end, we see him triumph over the earlier difficulties. In a list Adam made at the end of first grade of what he liked about school, he put writing at the very top.

Figure 4—1

Notes Figure 4—1 was the first book Adam wrote in first grade. He worked on it from early September until late November. He was the last child in his first-grade class to finish a book for "publication," which meant its being typed (by a parent) on good-quality paper, using conventional spelling and punctuation.

Adam's school schedule contained a thirty- to thirty-five-minute writing period

59

Figure 4–1   Adam's First Book in First Grade (Excerpts) (Age 6 Years, 2 Months to 6 Years, 5 Months)

A

B

C

each day, during which children were supposed to work on their books. Adam spent a lot of his time creating patterns out of colored parquetry blocks and then copying these onto graph paper. Only reluctantly, according to Adam's teacher, would Adam actually write words in his book.

Comments   It was clear during the first four months of Adam's year in first grade that his kindergarten honeymoon with writing was over. Now he agonized over his writing and said he "hated" doing it. He even said that he hated first grade, which I thought at first was simply a case of nostalgia for kindergarten. But when the feelings persisted beyond the first two or three weeks, I realized that something else must be at issue.

"Why do you hate first grade?" I asked.

"Because I hate to write!" came the answer.

"Why do you hate to write?" I asked him.

"Because I can't write. I don't know how to write. My words don't look right, no matter how hard I try to sound them out!"

At first, I didn't offer any specific or useful advice, thinking, I guess, that he was exaggerating his plight and that his negative attitude soon would pass. But it didn't.

A few days later, when he literally slumped into a heap on the living-room floor, sobbing uncontrollably, I realized that I needed to do something. I probed a bit to find out exactly what the problem was. When I asked him why he was so upset, he said, "Because I'm getting behind in my work." When I asked him what work he was getting behind in, he said, "My writing."

"And why is that?" I asked.

"Because I don't do my writing, because I can't make words the right way," he said.

"But can't you ask your teacher to help you?" I asked.

"No. He won't help us. He tells us to do them ourselves, to do the best we can."

"Oh," I said, as I continued to probe. "So you're afraid that after you go ahead and do them, he will be upset that they are wrong?"

"No," he cried out. "He doesn't *care* if they are right!"

"Then are you afraid that Mommy and Daddy will say that they aren't right?"

"No," he said, as he wailed even louder.

"Then why are you upset about how your words look?" I asked. "Why don't you just do them the best that you can?"

"Because I want to do them *right*!" he said, almost shouting in an attempt to make me understand.

"Oh," I said. "Well, I'll tell you what. When I want to make sure that I spell words right, I check a book called a dictionary." I went to my office to get my blue *Webster's*, which I consult regularly, and showed him this book with its thousands and thousands of words. He looked at it with an expression of utter fascination. "This dictionary would be a little hard for you to use," I explained, "because it has so many words in it. But we could make a dictionary for you by using a notebook and labeling it with all of the letters of the alphabet. Then you could tell me the words you want me to write in it. Do you want to make one?" I asked.

"Yes," he said enthusiastically.

"Luckily, I had an extra spiral notebook at home, which I had purchased for another purpose. We could use that one, I told Adam, and I went to get it. For the next forty-five minutes, we worked on the dictionary. Adam told me about twenty-five words that he wanted me to include. He insisted that I spell and write them. "I'll draw the pictures," he said. (He had decided that he'd need to draw a picture for each word, so that he could remember it.) (See **Figure 4–2.**)

As I wrote the first few entries, Adam watched intently. I noticed that he often looked puzzled. I noticed the expression once after I had entered the word "kite." It dawned on me that Adam couldn't figure out why I had added an *e* on the end, given that you don't hear it when you say the word.

"I bet you are wondering why I put an *e* on the end of that word, aren't you?" I said to him.

"Yes," he said. "I don't get it."

"Well, that *e* tells you how to pronounce the *i* in the middle of the word," I explained. "It's called 'silent *e*' because you don't say it when you say the word. It has a different job. It tells us to pronounce the word as 'kite' instead of as 'kit.'"

"So, if you didn't know about silent *e*, you'd just waste *k–i–t* when you wanted to spell 'kite.' Right?" Adam queried.

"That's right," I said.

In a moment Adam had grasped the reason for silent *e*: It made for a much more efficient system; otherwise you'd "waste *k–i–t* when you wanted to spell 'kite,'" as he had put it.

When we had finished making entries on this night, Adam packed the dictionary in his backpack, to take to school the next day. I warned him that I wasn't sure he'd be allowed to use it, but I promised to write a note to his

Figure 4–2 Adam's Dictionary (Excerpts)

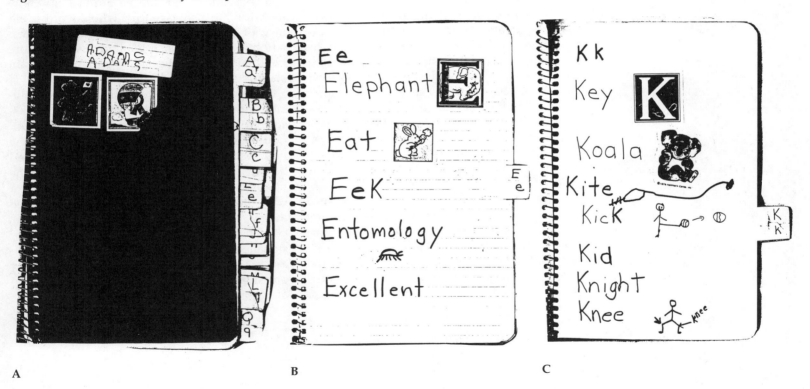

A   B   C

teacher to explain why I thought the dictionary was needed. I wrote the note, and Adam was allowed to use the dictionary.

We continued making dictionary entries every night after school over the next six or seven weeks. In fact, adding words to his dictionary was the first thing Adam wanted to do when he arrived home from school each day. I purchased some stickers that Adam could use in the place of hand-drawn pictures.

Gradually Adam's interest in adding new words to his dictionary waned, although he still kept it packed in his backpack and took it to school with him for many more weeks to come.

Adam's need for his dictionary lessened as the school year went on. This was not because he had learned the spellings of most of the words he needed. He hadn't, although his words were beginning to look better and better as he added more vowels in the words he generated by himself and also began to learn more and more words by sight. But even if they didn't look exactly right, he didn't get upset now that he knew spelling was hard and not simply a matter of coding the sounds heard. He *expected* that he would make mistakes, given what he now knew about spelling.

But things did not become quite this easy right away. At home, for a while, Adam still sometimes said that he didn't know how to write. He also asked for whole-word spellings or copied words from a known source. After a few months, he had become more independent, but he still asked how certain sounds were to be spelled.

He also seemed very involved in analyzing print whenever he saw it—on trucks, storefronts, magazine covers, and so on. Often, he would comment, "Oh, I didn't know you spelled —— like that," which indicated he was thinking about the spellings of the words that he saw and was comparing them with how he might have chosen to spell them.

This return to more dependent behavior signalled the dawning of a whole new spelling era for Adam. Far from indicating a regression in behavior, it marked the first step of a great leap forward.

Figure 4-3

Notes   Adam wrote what is shown in Figure 4-3A at home one day, late in September, just a few days after we had started the dictionary

project. He was sitting on the living-room
sofa, felt-tip marker in hand, writing on a
piece of paper. He sat for a long time, writing.
Often he'd pause to look at his paper, before
beginning to write again. I wondered what
was so absorbing, so I sat down next to him
and asked him what he was doing.

"Well, I'm writing letters and then seeing which ones I know the sound for," he
explained.

At that point he had crossed out the letters
H, K, C, Y, A, D, Z, N, M, B, R, T, G, and *S.* Left
uncovered were the letters *O* and *I.* "Oh," I
said, "you know, all of the letters you've crossed
out, except the *A*, are called 'consonants.' The
O and the *I*, which you haven't crossed out,
are vowels. So is *A*, but you know it because it
is in your name. Consonant sounds are easier
than vowel sounds to remember," I went on,
"because they usually just say one sound,
which you hear when you say their name." I
gave some examples, such as how we hear the
/m/ sound when we say the name of the letter
M, and how we hear the /s/ sound when we
say the letter *S*. "But vowels are a little different.
They make the sound heard when you say
their names, but they represent other sounds
too."

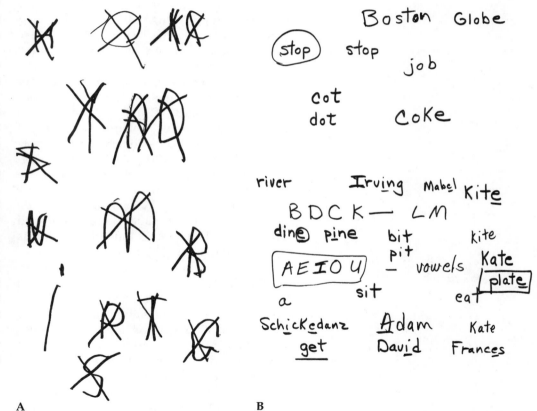

Figure 4–3   At Home (Age 6 Years, 2 Months). A: Letters. B: Words.

A

B

Then I reminded him that he really did know the sounds that these other vowels made, because he knew some words that had them in them. The first example I gave was the word "stop." "Oh, yeah," he said, as he placed a cross over the letter *O*. Then I gave him some other examples, including "Boston," "job," "cot," and "dot." Then I said, "The tricky part is knowing when an *O* in a word has one sound—its name—or the other sound. That's what's hard." Then I reminded him about the discussion of silent *e* we had had while working on his dictionary. Then I wrote two words, "Globe" (to go with Boston, because that's the name of the newspaper we get) and "Coke," to illustrate how the silent *e* marks an interior vowel for its long sound. By this time, his original paper had been flipped to the other side where I could write the words I was talking about (Figure 4–3B).

Then I went on to the letter *E*, reminding him that his grandmothers' names had *E*'s in them, and that they had the sound that *E* makes when it doesn't say its name. I wrote "Mabel" and "Frances" on the paper, underlining their *E*'s. I also wrote down the word "get" to provide another example.

Then we proceeded to the letter *I*, for which I provided our last name as a good prototype for the soft *I* sound. We noticed that "Schickedanz" also contains an *E* and an *A*. I added the words "David" and "Irving,"

Adam's father's first and last names, as other examples of words that contain a short *I* sound.

Then I wrote the word "river" to provide another example. Adam noticed that it also contained an *E*. "But not a long *E or* a short one," I explained. "You never hear the vowel when it comes before an *R*. You know it is there because every syllable must have a vowel; that's just a rule for making words."

I went on to remind him that a syllable is a part of a word, and gave him some examples, such as "Schick-e-danz" and "A-dam." Then we dissected "river," noting that it had two syllables, which is why it needed another vowel in addition to the *I* we could hear.

This discussion was followed again by one about silent *e*. I wrote down the words "kite," "pine," and "dine," underlining their silent *e*'s at the end, to give him some examples. Then I showed him another way to know if a vowel is to say its name or not. I wrote the word "eat," pointing out that we hear the *E*, which in this case says its name, while the *A* remains silent. "When two vowels are together like that," I explained, "you usually say just one, not both. We say that 'one does the talking while the other does the 'walking.'"

Next we played around with long and short *A*'s for a while. I used words such as "Kate" and "plate," because Adam was more familiar with thinking about short *A*'s, given their presence in his name.

Then I wrote all the vowels (except *Y*) in a row, to indicate that we had one more vowel left to discuss. But Adam said that we didn't need to do that. "I get it," he said. "Don't do any more."

Comments Apparently the discussions we'd had about why I wrote the words the way I did when I entered them in Adam's dictionary prompted Adam to think about some things. When he said that he didn't know the sounds of the letters he had not crossed out, I don't think he meant that he knew none *at all*. Instead, he had been thinking about the other sounds they make, the ones they make when there's not a silent *e* on the end of a word, such as "kite," which we had discussed several days previously in conjunction with the dictionary.

Now Adam was trying to figure out those other sounds that certain letters could make, and he thought he didn't know them, although he actually did, because he knew lots of words that contained them. But he had not thought much about vowels in these contexts; in fact, because they are not very dominant in words when we pronounce them, they often are not even represented in children's early spellings. Except for the short *A*, which Adam knew from his name (and perhaps heard in other words because of this), he typically did not represent the short vowels in words he generated with his sound-based spelling system.

Many children first represent these lax vowels by selecting the tense vowel with which the lax vowel shares the most phonetic features. But at first Adam did not do this, perhaps because his visual word knowledge created so much dissatisfaction with writing that he became upset and was unable to proceed. His upset then prompted me to help him make a dictionary, which, in turn, prompted me to explain myself when Adam looked puzzled about spellings. This explanation led to a discussion about silent *e* and a contrasting discussion about the other sounds that vowels can make. This explanation then prompted Adam to think about these other sounds that vowels can make and to explore these possibilities for representing new sounds he was beginning to hear, instead of searching among his current tense vowel list for a reasonable substitute.

Perhaps children who are content to use tense vowel substitutes for lax vowels have less visual information about words than Adam had, so they continue to write without becoming upset, in a way that Adam could not. Adam, too, would use the tense vowel substitution strategy in combination with some short vowel knowledge. It was as if, in thinking about which vowel to select to spell a sound, he sometimes searched his knowledge of short vowel words and sounds to arrive at a candidate, and at other times searched among his tense vowel list. This combined strategy is to be expected, I think, when a child has both kinds of information from which to work.

Figure 4—4

Notes Adam was invited to three birthday parties, all scheduled for one weekend in November. It was our custom for Adam to make the greeting card to accompany a child's gift. He needed to write three cards this time, one for each of his friends, Andrew, Sean, and Arash (Figure 4—4).

I told Adam that he needed to make the cards for the birthday gifts. I suggested that he write, "To ———," on the front of each piece of paper, which I already had folded in half to form the card; and that he add a message on the inside before writing "From Adam."

Adam wrote, "To Andro B" (Figure 4—4A —Andrew's last name began with a *B*) on the first card and then said, "I don't want to write the message; you do it." I agreed to help but told Adam he should decide what the message should say. "Happy Birthday," he dictated. I wrote it down. Then I handed the card back to Adam and said, "Now you write, 'From Adam.'" He took the pencil, wrote an *F* and an *R* as he sounded the word out, and then paused. "How do you write /uh/?" he asked. I told him that it is spelled with the letter *O*. He added this letter and then the final *M* before writing his name.

The second card he wrote was for Sean (Figure 4—4B). He wrote "To" and had pronounced the first phoneme of Sean's name. But before he had a chance to decide how to represent it, I said, "You need an *S*, even though it sounds like it should be *Sh*." Adam wrote the *S* and then wrote *O* to represent the middle sound before I had a chance to tell him that this part of Sean's name was spelled a little differently too. (Given that Adam already had written it his way, I let it stand without comment.) Then Adam added the final *N*.

When Adam wrote the message on the inside of Sean's card, he referred to the words "Happy Birthday" that I had written inside of Andrew's card and copied them.

Figure 4-4   Birthday Cards (Age 6 Years, 4 Months). A: Andrew's. B: Sean's. C: Arash's.

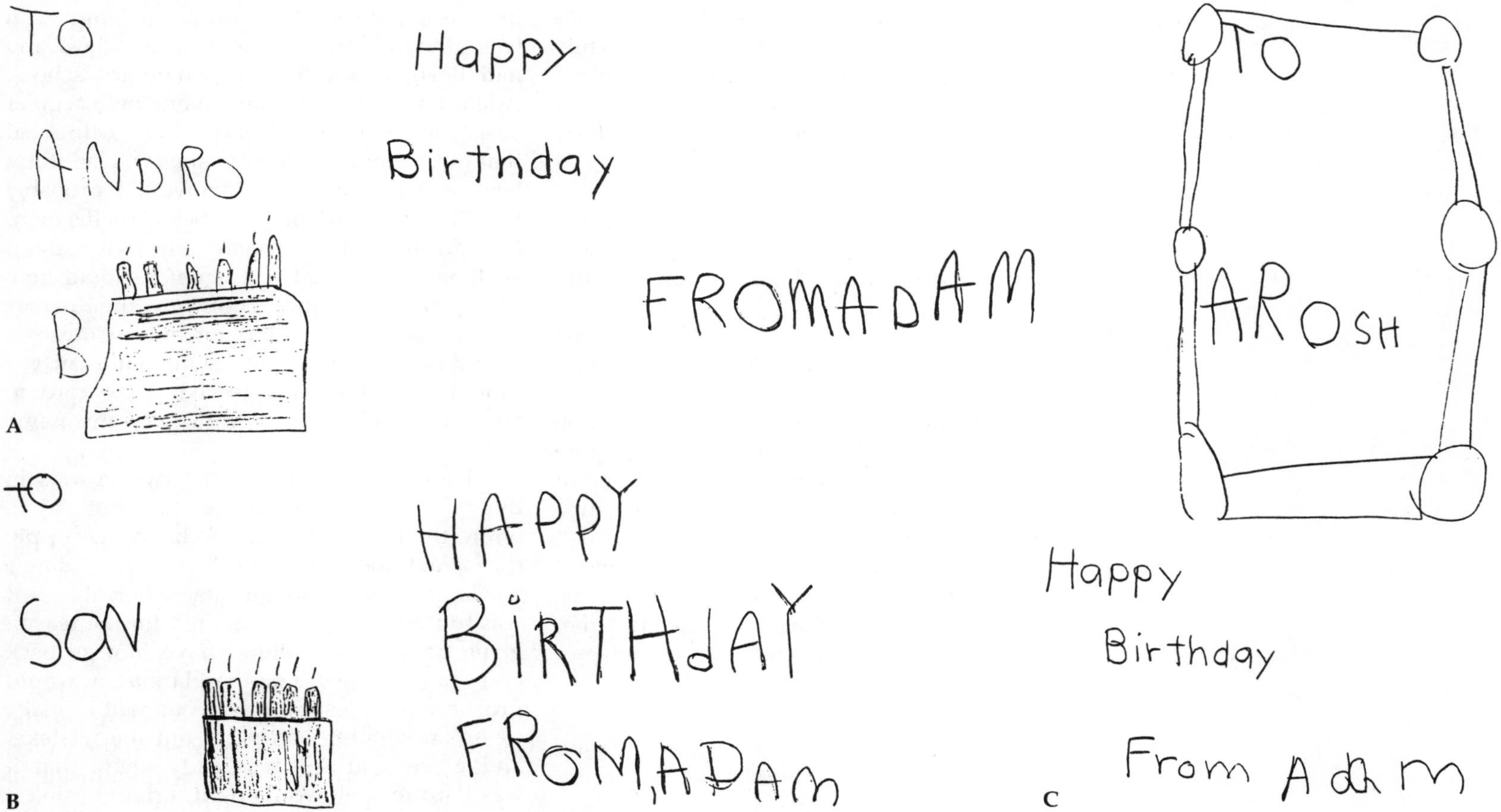

Adam spelled Arash's name on the front of the third card (Figure 4–4C) all by himself, representing the middle *A* with an *O*. Then he told me that he wanted me to write the message inside, because he wanted to watch television. (A favorite program had come on while we were writing the cards.) I agreed to write "Happy Birthday" and "From" but told Adam that he would need to sign his name, which he did.

Comments   On this occasion, we see some hesitancy toward writing, although it was easily overcome when I told Adam I would help.

It is interesting that Adam did not resist writing at the very beginning, with Andrew's name. I think he did not because he was fairly confident that he knew how to spell Andrew's name, which he had seen quite often in his nursery school class (a different Andrew) and kindergarten class (the same Andrew). The greeting, "Happy Birthday," was far less familiar to Adam visually, and it was here that Adam first balked. Adam was able to write the message the second time, when he could copy it from the model provided in the first card.

With Sean's name, I gave Adam the spelling for the first sound without waiting for him to get started. I did this because I knew that Adam was likely to spell the name incorrectly, given its unusual spelling. Sean was a friend from nursery school days and had been in a different elementary school. Adam had not seen Sean's name on a regular basis for about a year and a half. I doubted that he'd remember how to spell it. Had it not been a name that was involved, I probably would have let Adam spell "Sean" on his own. But given Adam's recent sensitivity about spelling words right, I thought I should help him out here. Children know how their names are spelled and might point out an error. It would be particularly devastating at a party, I thought, for the child receiving the card to announce, "Hey! You didn't spell my name right!"

I intended to supply the two vowels in the middle of Sean's name, too, but Adam wrote the *O* before I had a chance to supply the actual spelling. I decided to let Adam's spelling stand, although later when the card was finished, I wished I hadn't, for the reason given above. But I didn't have him go back and change it. Sean's mother, I thought, would probably have a supportive comment to make to Adam should Sean point out the mistake, and given that Adam already knew that it was hard to spell words right, I didn't think it would add greatly to his writing discomfort. This situation had, however, been the first for a very long time in which I had supplied any spelling information at all without first having been asked. But knowing what I did about Adam's conception of spelling at this point, it seemed an appropriate thing to do. On the one hand, I knew the information would not be rejected. I also felt it would not undercut Adam's independence.

But I was selective in the information I gave. I didn't want to dictate all of the spellings because this approach could have had the effect of undercutting Adam's independence. A little unsolicited information sprinkled here and there would serve as help, would actually preserve Adam's independent action. More information, I thought, might go beyond the point of serving as support. It might look more like a takeover, which I wanted to avoid.

When teaching, we always do a balancing act with the many values and goals we have in mind. Almost always, a specific act of teaching can both advance one goal while pushing another backward. It is for this reason that we must choose carefully what we will do and when we will do it. I chose to help Adam with Sean's name because an incorrect spelling here was likely to have some negative consequences. And I gladly helped him with the spellings of "Happy Birthday" and the middle sound in the word "from," which he requested. But the rest was left to Adam, and the overriding message I tried to convey from the beginning was, "You are able to write these birthday cards."

Figure 4—5

Notes The first really independent writing Adam did again at home is shown in Figure 4—5. These were Christmas lists. Adam wrote the words first and then drew the pictures, a complete reversal of the approach he took for his birthday list some nine months earlier. When finished, he gave the list to me, read each item, and announced, "That's what I want."

Comments There are many conventional spellings in this gift list, including "Legos," "cobra," and "gun." The word "Transformer" ("TRANSFORMR") is spelled almost correctly except for the omission of the vowel before the final *R*. The other words contain more errors but are quite fleshed out, which no doubt made them look right to Adam.

Figure 4–5   Christmas Lists (Age 6 Years, 5 Months)

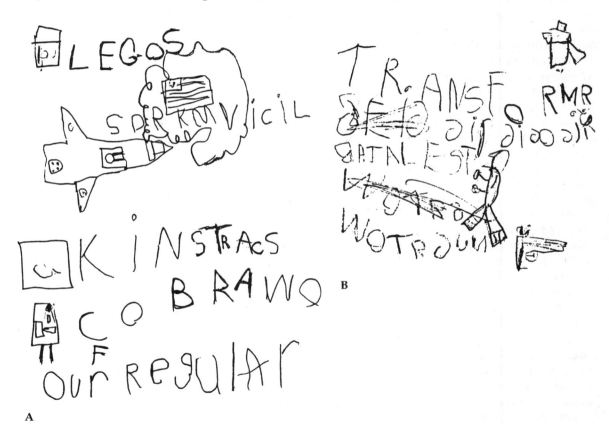

A

B

Adam had crossed out some errors himself. The first of these occurred when he attempted to write "G.I. Joe," (Figure 4–5B), which he spelled out more fully than is needed. Adam first wrote *GE*, representing both the phoneme represented by *G* as well as the long *E* he also heard. Then he recorded an *i* for the *I*, which comes after the *G* in the name "G.I. Joe." Then he recorded a *G*, the beginning sound in the word "Joe." However, at this point, he apparently remembered how he had seen this word spelled on toys, so he crossed it out and started over. This time, he used just a *G* and an *I* for "G.I." before adding a *G* and an *O* to spell "Joe." What looks like a second writing of "G.I." actually was placed there as part of the picture. He drew a figure and then placed the *G* and *I* in front of it to indicate what kind of figure it was.

Adam's second correction came when he tried to write the words "water" and "gun." The small curved part of the first *G* he had made for the word "gun" had been closed, making it look like a lowercase *A* or an inverted lowercase *E*. I wondered at first why Adam had not let the word "water" stay there, while he merely crossed out his incorrect *G* at the beginning of the word "gun." Then it occurred to me that, to Adam, "water" and "gun" probably were not conceptualized as two words; they were just one. So the whole thing had to be crossed out, given that Adam

thought his mistake had occurred in the middle of the word, not at the beginning.

Figure 4–6

Notes The writing shown in Figure 4–6 was taken from three books that Adam wrote at school between January and March of first grade. I didn't see the books in the process of being written. They stayed at school while Adam wrote them and stayed there a while longer to allow the teacher time to read them with Adam. Still more time elapsed between the time they were finished and the time they were given to the parent volunteer, who prepared their published versions. The story about the wrestling match (Figure 4–6C) was not published but apparently sat in Adam's cubby drawer for several weeks before he brought it home.

Between the samples shown in Figures 4–6A and 4–6B, Adam wrote another story, "The Day that It Snowed." For some reason, only the final published version, which I typed, made it back home. Therefore, I can't recapture the way Adam first wrote it. But while I was typing his book, he watched.

Figure 4-6 Three Books (Age 6 Years, 7 Months to 6 Years, 9 Months). A: O BOY BRiTHR. B: THE MONSTR. C: THE RESSALENG MACH.

O BOY BRiTHR

WNSTHEREWiSABRiTHANDASISTER

(Once there was a brother and a sister.)

THERNAMSWRSERiANDPTR

(Their names were Sara and Peter.)

PTRWASABADBRATHR

(Peter was a bad brother.)

HESCERDACAT

(He scared a cat.)

HIS SSTRLOCTATHIM

(His sister looked at him.)

HESEDIiMSREOBOW

(He said, "I'm sorry." Oh, boy!)

HE WAS TUgENg ON HIS SISTRS CATS TEAL.

A (He was tugging on his sister's cat's tail.)

HIS SISTR YE1SAT HRBRAThR

(His sister yells at her brother.)

HeOLMOST CiLDA giNEPig iFHeDiDNT FOL

(He almost killed a guinea pig, if he didn't

fall.) (Meaning i̶t̶ he would have if he hadn't fallen

before jumping on it, which was shown in the illustration.)

He COTTHe BRK OF THE TRE

(He cut the bark off the tree.)

HIS MOM TOLDHiM TO STOP iT. OK

(His mom told him to stop it, "Okay?")

He WenT APSTERs TOHiS ROM

(He went upstairs to his room.)

HE WAS NOT HAPE.

(He was not happy.)

HE HEDBIN SCOLDiD Bi His MOM.

(He had been scolded by his mom.)

SOHE WAS NiSTO ANAMALS AND NACHR

(So he was nice to animals and nature.)

THE MONSTR

THE MONSTR iS GiTENG OT AV HiS SHiP

(The monster is getting out of his ship.)

THE MONSTR iS WOKEN To HiS BAS

(The monster is walking to his bas.)

THE MONSTR iS NER THE BAS

(The monster is walking to his bas.)

THE MONSTR iS iN HiS BAS

(The monster is in his bas.)

THE MONSTR iS GOENG TO RTh

(The monster is going to earth.)

B   THE END

THE RESSALENG MACH

(The Wrestling Match)

THE NOKOT iS GOD

(The knockout is good.)

THEr BEEng BETiD UP

(They are being beated up.)

HE iS HODENG HiS NEC

(He is holding his neck.)

THE Gi ON THE LET iS HOLDEN THE GiS PUNCH

(The guy on the left is holding the guy's punch.)

HE NOKS HiM OT

(He knocks him out.)

THEr iS A NOKOT FOR ECH 1.

(There is a knockout for each one.)

THA R SHACENG HANS

(They are shaking hands.)

THE MACH iS OVR

C   (The match is over.)

When I spelled "snowed" Adam said, "Oh, you put a *W* in there and I didn't. I didn't know it had one."

I think it was also with this book that Adam first noticed the spaces between words. He didn't mention it to me, but his teacher told me to ask him about it. When I did, Adam said that he had wondered at first why I "wasted" all of that space when I typed his story. His teacher had explained that this strategy makes it easier for someone else to read what you've written. That was a "good idea," Adam told me. "I'm going to do that." We can see that he did, for in Figure 4–6B he has consistently inserted spaces between words.

Comments   Adam's calm reaction to the discovery that he had misspelled the word "snowed" stood in marked contrast to his reactions three to four months earlier. Now he expected that he would often spell words incorrectly because he knew that it was difficult to spell words right. In fact, I think he was observing me type his story so that he could see the difference between his spellings and my own. The behavior also contrasted sharply with his behavior about a year earlier, when we had worked together on his Apple Eater book. Then he hadn't seemed even to notice that the two of us spelled words differently.

The writing samples shown in Figure 4–6 seem to call into question the effectiveness of the instruction I gave Adam when I helped him with his dictionary and when I explained long and short vowels, silent e's, double vowels, and the need to include a vowel before an *R*. There are many instances where he did not seem to organize his behavior in terms of what I thought I had helped him understand.

For example, one thing he did not have under control at this point was knowledge of the correct letter to use when confronted with a lax vowel phoneme. Instead of searching through his known words to locate an appropriate exemplar from which to figure out the letter he needed, Adam often searched his list of tense vowels and chose one whose features were the closest to the sound he needed to represent. Adam used this strategy when he used an *I* to spell the words "was," "brother," and "Sara," in his "O Boy BriThr" story. He also used an *E* in the words "scared," "Sara," and "said" because the *A*'s there represent lax sounds that overlap the most with the phonetic features heard in the tense vowel represented by the letter *E*.

However, we also see several instances of correct representation of lax vowels, such as when he spelled the words "a," "and," "bad," "cat," and "at" and the words "his," "sister," "him," and "didn't."

We can see, as well, that Adam spelled the same word differently in different parts of the same story. For example, the words "was," "sister," and "boy" are spelled correctly sometimes and incorrectly other times. Some words are represented incorrectly in two different ways ("BRiTHR" and "BRATHR" for "brother").

There also were many instances where Adam did not use the knowledge that every syllable must have a vowel. But I don't think the instruction I gave him earlier was totally disregarded. Though Adam was not able to utilize the information completely during the writing of a first draft, when he had to compose, record, and illustrate a story, Adam's writing bore some mark of our discussion. Some of the information was being used some of the time; and this, given how much there is to understand, is all that can be expected.

The children in Adam's first-grade classroom were not asked to read over and edit their stories until the very end of the school year, when each child wrote an Egyptian myth in conjunction with a unit on Ancient Egypt. The process his teacher used for this writing project had three steps:

1. A first draft was done on wide-lined primary paper, the kind of paper on which the children had written all of their previous stories.

2. The story was then rewritten in a second "practice book," after the child and the teacher had discussed the first draft and had identified and corrected the misspellings. The corrected version was then rewritten in the practice book, which was smaller than the first-draft book and contained paper with no lines. At this stage, the child worked on reducing the size of the writing and tried to get it organized well on the page. Correct spellings also were to be incorporated.

3. When step 2 had been completed, the child was given a final book, a book whose pages had decorations in the four corners. This was the copy that would sit atop the piano on the day that the classroom's Ancient Egyptian museum would be open for parents to tour.

Adam loved working on his Egyptian myth book. He never complained about the work. In fact, he said in very enthusiastic tones that he "was going to be ready for my practice book very soon" and then that he had been given "my final, final, final, special book to write my myth in."

I don't know if all of the children were ready to undertake their own editing and publishing. If they weren't, I suspect that the process was tedious, frustrating, and numbing. But Adam was ready, and the work elevated, instead of lowered, his interest in writing.

Figure 4–7

[ ]

Notes Adam created the book shown in Figure 4–7 on a Saturday, one week after the end of first grade. He had gone with me to the Boston University Nursery School, where I wanted to feed the fish, water the plants, and do a few other odd tasks, before settling firmly into the July Fourth weekend.

When I unlocked the door to the school, Adam immediately headed for the classroom writing center. I must have been working for at least half an hour when Adam brought the book shown in Figure 4–7 to me. "Here's a present for you, Mom," he said. "Read it." I did.

Comments I noticed several things about Adam's writing in his book, including the accurate use of *U* in the words "sun," "up," and "fun." He also used *I* accurately to represent the lax vowel sound in the words "it," "is," and "winter," and he had spelled correctly the -ing ending of the word "writing," although he hadn't generalized this notion to other words (e.g., "reading" and "playing").

Adam had also added vowels before the *R*'s in the last syllables of the words "summer" ("Somer"), "winter," and "soccer" ("Socer"); and he had applied his knowledge of double vowels to represent the tense vowel sound in the words "reading" ("Readeang"), "snowing" ("Snoweeng"), "playing" ("Plaeeng"), and "recess" ("reases"). Perhaps he had seen the word "writing" more often than the others, so he fashioned its ending from visual knowledge. The other -ing words, however, were generated by paying attention to the tense vowel and then trying to apply his double-vowel knowledge to this situation. Not a bad strategy, to be sure, but something that

Figure 4–7   Adam's Book (Age 7 Years)

A

The sun is up It is Somer!

B

It is Snoweery. It is winter.

C

Wot i lic
Obot SHool
Riting readeang
Math renses
bonch Gym.

they are fun?

D

continued

Figure 4–7 Continued

E

I lic plaeeng Socer.

F

I lic plaeeng. The end

G

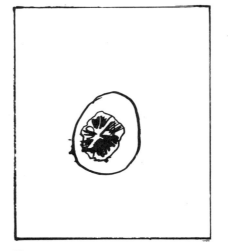

H

would need to be straightened out (which happened when he realized the similarity among these words and began to apply -ing to all of them).

Adam also had added two punctuation marks to his writing in Figure 4–7. This was something that had first appeared in his school stories, though only very occasionally (see Figure 4–6). In Figure 4–7, he used a period at the end of every sentence, except the first one on the first page ("The sun is up") and the second sentence on that page, where he used an exclamation point instead.

Adam omitted the colon and the commas that were needed on his "What I like about school" page (Figure 4–7D), I think because placing punctuation here did not fit his rule. I think his rule at this point was to put a period at the end of every thought, unless you were excited; then an exclamation point should be used. (Was this his understanding of having been told, perhaps at school, to put a period at the end of every sentence?) Apart from this rule, I think Adam was quite unaware of the need for punctuation. Even in his reading behavior, at this point, I noticed that he often overran pauses (commas) and had just begun to self-correct overruns on full stops (periods),

when doing so left what he had just read not making sense. Perhaps it was from his reading that he was beginning to get some ideas about the need for punctuation. Or perhaps his rule had come from the editing work that he had done on his Egyptian myth in his first-grade classroom.

I must admit, however, that what I noticed first about this piece of writing was the fact that writing topped Adam's list of things that he liked about school. He had come a long way from the early days of first grade when writing was something that he hated to do. Now that he knew more about writing, he liked to write.

"The Things I Told My Friend"

A Summary of Adam's Word-Creation Hypotheses

The preceding chapters have focused on the development of Adam's ideas about writing. To summarize his long journey, in this chapter I have created some fictional bits of conversation like those I think Adam would have had with a friend, had he been able to conceptualize and talk about what he was learning.

Of course it was impossible for Adam to have such conversations while he made most of his journey. Very young children aren't very good at understanding what they understand or at explaining to others what they know. This is why it is difficult to teach children of this age. They can't tell us what they don't know or what confuses them. We have to listen; observe; and, yes, even guess. But by digging up fossils, as it were, and by going through artifacts, such as samples of a child's writing, we can begin to piece together the skeleton of a child's development.

The bit of fiction that follows is an attempt to put flesh on these bones in order to create a more complex picture of what life at important junctures must have been like for Adam.

Age Two Years, Eight Months

"You can draw words, if you want to. But when you want to make a word, you have to try to make it go with the person or thing it stands for. If it's a big thing, make a long word. If it's a little thing, make it a short word. If the word is you, make just enough marks to match how old you are."

Age Two Years, Nine Months

```
┌─────────────────────────────────────┐
│                                     │
└─────────────────────────────────────┘
```

"Forget about matching words with the size or age of something. That's not how you are supposed to do it. There's this design that people use to write the name of each thing, and it doesn't even look like the thing. You just have to try to make your design when you want to write your name. And if you want to write somebody else's name, you have to write their design. If you can't make the whole design for something, that's okay. Just make as much of it as you can and then fill in the empty spaces with marks that are sort of like what belongs there."

Age Two Years, Ten Months

```
┌─────────────────────────────────────┐
│                                     │
└─────────────────────────────────────┘
```

"You know, you can say words *or* you can write them. Well, they are the same word, whichever way you do it, but they go together, so when you write it you have to make it sort of like when you say it. So if the word has two beats, then you need to make two marks. But if it has three beats, then you need three. You can write all the words you need this way. You don't have to learn a new design for each one."

Age Three Years, Six Months

```
┌─────────────────────────────────────┐
│                                     │
└─────────────────────────────────────┘
```

"Know what? If you want to write words, forget about how words sound; the important thing is how they look. If you want to make a word, just put some letters together in a line. You have to use enough, but not too many. For example, two wouldn't be enough, and ten, I think, would be too many. Maybe five would be good. And you have to use different ones; you can't have all the same kind in a word, because that doesn't look right. I don't think you are supposed to have more than two of one kind next to each other, at least this is what I've noticed. And if you want to make more words, you can use the same letters over again, if you remember to mix them up.

"If you want to know what words you've made when you're all done playing, just ask a grown-up. They know all of the words and can tell you which ones you made."

Age Four Years

[ ]

"Forget about trying to make words by just making sure they look right. Words are very tricky; sometimes letters look like they should make a word, but they don't. If you are trying to write a certain word, just ask a grown-up how to spell it. If you just want to play around with writing words and you want them to be real ones, look around on the classroom attendance chart, at the titles of some of your favorite books, or at labels your teacher has posted on things in the room.

"If you're at home, you can ask your mom to spell some words for you, because she's nice and has time. But don't ask your teacher; she'll just ask you what you think or will tell you to do it yourself, because she's too busy to help you. I don't think teachers like to help children with their words. But they don't mind tying their shoes. I have Velcro so I don't need help with my shoes. I think teachers should tell those other kids to get Velcro and to stop bothering them. Then they'd have time to help me spell words.

"When people tell you how to spell a word, try to remember it, because you'll probably need it again. And there are lots of words you are going to have to remember, so pay attention hard."

Age Four Years, Six Months

"Guess what? You don't have to learn how to spell every word. There's a shortcut. I noticed that grown-ups use certain letters when a word they are spelling starts with a certain sound. I thought about this one day, when my mom was telling me how to spell 'Voltron,' and she made this /v/ sound for a long time while she waited for me to tell her what letter I thought the word should start with. It sounded like the letter *V* to me, so I said '*V*,' and she said, 'Hey, that's right. The letter *V* makes the /v/ sound.' After that, I thought about this a little bit and I noticed that *B* makes the /b/ sound, *A* makes the /a/ sound, and *D* makes the /d/ sound. So I wrote a word using this idea and I took it to my mom and said, 'Hey, guess what word I wrote?' And she said, 'Let me see: S−P−R−M−N. I think it says "Superman."' And she was right! So now I can write words all by myself, and I don't have to ask anybody to help me. Writing is sooooo easy!"

Age Six Years

"Hey, you know, some of the sounds in words are really hard to hear. I didn't used to think that anything was there, but there really is. So listen really hard, or you won't be able to spell words right. And then ask your mom what letter to use for the sound. Or pick out another letter from the ones you use to write some other sounds. Think about which of the letters you know sounds the most like this new sound you want to write, and use it. But be careful. It's got to look right."

Age Six Years, Six Months

┌─────────────────────────────────┐
│   │
└─────────────────────────────────┘

"Know what? Now the problem is that I just found out that every word has to have a vowel in each syllable and that you're supposed to know which vowel makes those sounds you can't hear very well. You aren't supposed to just listen and pick a close relative.

"And then you have to be able to tell people if this *I* or *E* you have decided to write down should be one sound or the other, because those letters can have two different sounds, you know, and you might not be there to tell them which one, if you mailed it to them in a letter or something like that. So you have to use these clues, like in a mystery when there are hints about who did the killing or stealing or whatever crime it was. Well, it's like that when you write. You have to give people clues. Now, there's the silent *e* clue and the double-vowel clue and more, I think, but I don't know all of them yet. But when you use these, they tell the person to say the letter with its name or with that other sound the letter can say.

"So, see, if you want to write 'kite,' you don't have to waste the word 'kit' and do something all different. And you don't have to just be confusing to somebody either. You can put an *E* on the end of the word, because that's a clue about how they should say the *I*.

"See how this works? It's really awesome that writing is like a mystery with clues and everything, but I hope there aren't too many. And I hope I don't learn anything else about writing, because it is getting too hard for me, and I bet you are getting tired of all of these corrections. Well, I don't think there will be too many more, maybe none, so don't worry. Okay?"

two

Connections

I n this part, I discuss connections—the implications of Adam's story, what it means. First, I try to determine the extent to which Adam's behavior was unique. Was he the only child whose early writing development took this particular course, or was his behavior fairly typical? I explore these questions in Chapter 6, "Research Connections."

Second, I try to determine the reasons for Adam's development, the forces that propelled it forward. Did his ideas simply unfold from within, or were specific experiences responsible for moving him along? These questions are explored in Chapter 7, "Theory Connections."

Finally, in Chapter 8, I discuss teaching connections. Among other things, I consider the factors that influence our intervention in children's learning and how these operate in the different contexts of home and school.

CHAPTER

6 Research Connections

The story of Adam, reported in Part I, is a case study. While case studies can provide an extremely detailed understanding of one child, their generalizability is severely limited. In the absence of confirming data from other children, we cannot know if the one case is an anomaly or if the behavior fits a more general rule. This problem decreases a study's usefulness, because we cannot know if insights gleaned apply to any more than this one child.

Because of this methodological problem, I was delighted when Adam's behavior reminded me of another child I had known. And I was thrilled when research reports of other children contained data that were similar to my own. I review some of these data in this chapter. I haven't tried, however, to provide an exhaustive review of the literature on emergent literacy. My purpose is not to present a comprehensive picture of how Adam's early literacy

development compared with that of other children. I want simply to show that similarities exist between Adam's behavior and the behavior of other children, that the course of his early literacy development was not unique.

Other Children Create First Words That Relate Physically to Their Referents

When Adam first wrote his name at the age of two years, eight months, he tried to maintain a physical relationship between his age and the number of marks he used. Several researchers have observed similar behavior in other children.

In the studies of literacy development conducted by Emilia Ferreiro and Ana Teberosky (1982), several children assumed that the length of a word should correspond to the size or age of the object or person it represented. One four-year-old, for example, said that the word "bear" (*oso* in Spanish) should be longer than the word for duck. When asked why, he explained that this was necessary because a bear is bigger than a duck. Similarly, a five-year-old said that writing about his papa would need to be longer than writing about his brother, presumably because his father was older. And a second five-year-old said that her name needed to be longer today than yesterday, because she'd just had a birthday (pp. 180, 184).

Two Swiss researchers, Papandropoulou and Sinclair (1974), also documented the young child's tendency to unite physical characteristics of a thing with characteristics of the word they create to represent that thing. For example, children suggested that long words should go with long or big objects or with actions that take a long time. Short words, on the other hand, should go with small objects, and so on. In their study, children as old as four and a half or five held such assumptions about the nature of words.

These data suggest that this hypothesis is fairly common among children who are just beginning to think about written language. Adam was not unique in using it. However, there is a striking age discrepancy between Adam and the other children whose behavior is cited in the literature. Adam used this hypothesis just once, as far as I know, at the age of two years, eight months. In contrast, the children whose behavior is described by other researchers were four and five years old.

Other Children Create Words by Trying to Recreate Visual Designs

When Adam stopped trying to maintain a physical relationship between words and their referents, he adopted a completely arbitrary approach to word-making. He simply set out to learn the specific design or pattern of letters that he had seen people associate with him. If they said that $A-D-A-M$ said Adam, then he would accept this and try to write it.

Marcia Baghban (1979) provides examples of her daughter, Giti, writing her name around the age of two years, six months. She doesn't mention any earlier attempts when Giti tried to make her name match her physical size or age, so it is difficult to know if Giti entertained this idea prior to the time that she began to try to write her name using the design that others used.

The young three-year-olds who attend the Boston University Preschool often seem to operate with a visual-design concept of word-making. Usually, it is their name that they are most interested in learning how to write. Occasionally, they are interested in another child's name, or in words such as "Mommy" and "Daddy." At this early stage, they seem to have no awareness that different words have some things in common—for example, that they contain common letters in different orders. Instead, they see each word as having a unique design, one that is arbitrarily assigned to stand for a given object or person.

Ferreiro and Teberosky (1982) refer to children's use of "stable strings." These essentially are sight words, words for which children know the order of the letters. Ferreiro and Teberosky discuss stable strings along with their discussion of mock words—words created by using visual rules. We saw that Adam varied some of the stable strings he knew—"Adam," "Mama"—when he was creating words based on visual rules (see Figure 2–4). However, he had learned at least one stable string—his name—long before he used it as a base from which to create variations. At this early point, which I call the visual-design stage, Adam had no idea of any general visual rules. His notion about words during this early period was that each one was totally arbitrary and unique, not related to any other words. Because Ferreiro and Teberosky studied children who were four, five, and six years of age, it is possible that they missed seeing children when they hold this assumption. However, they did observe children using the

physical-relationship hypothesis, a strategy Adam used prior to his use of visual designs. Perhaps Ferreiro and Teberosky's methodology, which involved the administration of tasks at fairly infrequent intervals, rather than the analysis of a continuous stream of spontaneously created writing samples, did not allow them to detect a unique period when children use a visual-design approach to word-making.

Other Children Use a Syllabic Strategy to Create Words

When Adam was about two years, ten months, he coded his name and several messages syllabically. The tendency for children to approach writing—and reading—with the assumption that individual written marks represent syllables has been noted by many researchers. Ferreiro and Teberosky (1982, p. 199) provide several examples. One four-year-old wrote *AO* when asked to write the word *oso*, a two-syllable Spanish word meaning "bear." A six-year-old in the same study wrote *AO* for *sapo*, which also has two syllables and means "toad." Other researchers, including Sulzby and Teale (1985) and Harste, Burke, and Woodward (1981), also have documented this behavior. In one example provided by Harste et al. (p. 78), a child named Lisa wrote "My name is Lisa." This is how she wrote it:

My name is Lisa.

Use of the syllabic hypothesis to create words is one of the most widely reported emergent literacy behaviors. Yet there is a discrepancy between my data and the data reported by other researchers, with respect to the exact behavior that should be considered representative of syllabic coding. Because we differ on this point, it is not surprising that the ages reported in other research differ markedly from the age at which I report that Adam used this hypothesis.

Ferreiro and Teberosky consider use of the syllabic hypothesis to be "Level 3" behavior. In their scheme, Level 2 behavior is characterized by a visual approach, one in which rules about minimum and maximum numbers of characters, and variability, are used to create letter strings that children think are words. Adam, as well as other children I have observed in the preschool at Boston University, exhibited these two behaviors in the opposite order: Letter strings — mock words — based on a visual-rule hypothesis appear *after* children create words by coding their beats with one mark each.

The discrepancy in our ordering of children's word-creation strategies could be due to actual differences among the children we have observed. Our populations are different in terms of nationality and social class. However, I suspect that the differences resulted from our use of different definitions, or narrower (my) versus broader (their) views about the type of behavior that should be included in this category.

Unlike Ferreiro and Teberosky, I restricted the use of the syllabic hypothesis to writing samples in which Adam used only as many characters as were needed to code the syllables. If he used more, then I decided that he was not simply using the syllabic hypothesis but was combining strategies perhaps by carrying over a learned design for a word, such as his name. Sometimes, even when it appeared that just one letter was used to represent each syllable, I disqualified the behavior as syllabic coding. I did this when letters used to code were selected correctly and systematically in terms of their conventional sound values. When letters are selected in terms of specific sounds, a child is not thinking, or perhaps does not mean to code, in terms of syllables. In some of these instances, Adam made what I have called recording errors: He failed to record as many sounds as he heard and intended to record.

An example of this kind of coding, which at first seemed to be syllabic, appeared on a page of his Apple Eater book. He wrote:

HEWGTiDiNiMNiT

His message—both as he said it out loud before recording and as he read it later—was: "He was going to get married in a minute." When Adam reread his story, he knew instantly that he had left something out, that he hadn't written all that he had intended to write. For the words he had wanted to write, these are the letters he actually had written down:

He was going to get married in a minute.

We can see that Adam wrote the words "he" and "in" in full; that he coded the words "was," "going," "to," "get," and "married," with just one letter each; and that he wrote the word "minute" by coding almost all of its sounds. If we took this sample at its face value, we could conclude that syllabic coding predominated, for indeed he had coded five of the five one-syllable words with just one letter each and had used just one letter to code two of the two-syllable words, making it appear that he had coded just one of their two syllables. However, when Adam

reread the story and realized that he had "left some parts out," here's what he told me to write down (shown inside the parentheses):

He W(as) G(oing) T(o) (G)i(t) (MRE)D iN i MNiT

For the words "was" and "going," Adam told me to "finish them." Then he offered the *o* to finish the word "to," the *G* and the *t* for the word "get," and the *M*, *R*, and *E* to complete the word "married."

We can see, then, that although Adam at first coded his message using what looked like predominantly a syllabic hypothesis, his *conceptualization* of the process went well beyond such a notion. His first coding was full of recording errors, which result when a child doesn't write down all of the sounds that he or she actually hears and intends to record, probably because the coordination demands required in the task are enormous for a beginning writer. (See pp. 54−55 for a discussion of what is involved.)

The tendency of Ferreiro and Teberosky not to distinguish conceptualization from recording could account for the differences between their data and mine. Given their broader definition of what syllabically generated writing entails, they included samples from a later time frame than my coding system would allow.

Due to my focus on conceptualization, I hesitated to categorize as syllabic any coding that involved correct and systematic selection of letters whose conventional sound values match the beginning sound found in the syllable being coded. If the correspondence is accidental, such as when a child like Adam uses *A* and *O* (his placeholder for *D*, which he called "D") to code his name, I counted the sample as an example of syllabic coding, because the child did not systematically select the letters. Adam, for example, used these two letters to code his name for a while because they were in his name and were the only ones he knew how to write at the time (see Figure 1–5). He used the same two letters to write his "Dear Mommy, I love you" messages, which indicated, without a doubt, that he was using letters from his limited repertoire rather than selecting letters for their sound value.

These stringent criteria, I think, make my results conflict with those of Ferreiro and Teberosky, as well as with those of Sulzby and Teale (1985), who provide a sample of writing created by a five-year-old, an age that matches more closely the children discussed by Ferreiro and Teberosky. The sample they provide is as follows (p. 3):

I wanted to ride a Big Wheel because

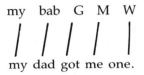

my dad got me one.

Each letter used is the conventional one for the first sound in the word being coded, assuming, as I think we can, that the child confused *d* and *b*. This is clearly a child who has some conscious awareness of phonemes (which the authors acknowledge in their discussion) and some specific letter-sound knowledge.

If we look closely at the sample, we also see that one two-syllable word ("because") is coded with three letters, not two. Two words ("my" and "dad") are spelled in full, with two and three letters respectively, despite the fact that each has but one syllable. And one two-syllable word ("wanted") is spelled with just one letter, not the two it should have if the child were using a syllabic coding system.

To me, this child is well beyond pure and simple syllabic coding. Some sight words (e.g., "my" and "dad") are included, one word ("because") is coded phonemically, with the three consonant sounds being represented, which is typical at the very beginning of independent invented spelling; and all of the other words except "one" are coded with the one letter that is the conventional letter used to represent the sound heard at the beginning of each word. For all we know, this child, like Adam, made some recording errors and for this reason failed to write down all of the sounds that he heard and meant to represent. The message in this case is quite long, which is exactly the context in which Adam was most likely to make a recording error.

Furthermore, we can't know for sure what the child had in mind when he used just the beginning letter to code so many of the words. Maybe this was a sort of shorthand to him, a quick way to get down and remember what his message was. This can be called a syllabic way of coding, I suppose, when the words are monosyllabic, but it is far different from what I have called Adam's syllabic coding, when he had not the foggiest notion that any particular letter could or should be used to code specific sounds. In other words, it's far different to code syllabically when syllables are the only sound segment of which you are aware than it is to make a conscious decision to code with just one letter because you find this approach easier than coding with more. Such a decision suggests possible knowledge of the idea of initials, which might be extended by children to whole sentences.

For example, on the cover of Adam's Sun Book (Figure 3–16), which he wrote when he was five years, ten months of age, he had written the letters *ADS*. When I saw this, I wondered if Adam was going to resume coding only syllables, this time using letters selected for their sound value. But when I asked Adam to tell me about the writing on the cover of his book, he said, "Oh, those are my initials."

I hadn't even known that Adam knew what initials are, so it hadn't occurred to me that these letters might be initials. Although Adam never wrote whole sentences in this abbreviated form (that I know of) it wouldn't have surprised me if he had. Children often overgeneralize an idea. A child might find it interesting or fun to write a sentence "using its initials."

In another example, this one provided by Harste, Burke, and Woodward (1981, p. 77), a child named Zach wrote this:

I like to play with my toys.

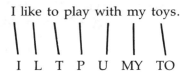

I   L   T   P   U   MY   TO

Zach paused and said, "That doesn't look long enough." At this point, he added an *A* and a *Q* to the *T* and *O* that he had used to code the last word, "toys." Zach, as it turns out, was not using pure syllabic coding. He was also guided visually, by the way words should look (i.e., longer). We can also see the influence of this visual strategy in his spelling of the word "my."

In addition, with but one exception (*U* for "with"), Zach selected letters that are used in conventional writing to code the first phoneme that appears in the words he wanted to write. Conceptually, then, he was thinking about phonemes, even though he recorded only one for most words, making it appear that he was thinking in terms of syllables. It would be interesting in such cases to probe a bit, to try to find out why a child who is clearly able to isolate phonemes codes only one rather than more.

In short, despite discrepancies in the behavior that researchers have categorized as syllabic coding, there is wide agreement in the literature that young children often use a syllabic hypothesis to generate the words they write. Once again, then, we see that Adam's behavior was not unique.

Other Children Use Visual Rules to Create Words

When using a visual-rule strategy to create words, children are concerned with how words look. They control the number of characters included in a word and also make certain that they vary. Furthermore, they think that by reordering a small set of letters, many different words can be made.

This approach to word-making has been observed by a variety of researchers (Pick et al. 1979; Clay 1975; Genishi and Dyson 1984; Ferreiro and Teberosky 1982). Some of these researchers also reported the question that Adam asked ("What word is this?"), while others noted that children attributed their own meanings to the words they created. For example, Clay (1975) describes one situation in which a child wrote several letter strings which she said were her dolls' names.

Reports of different researchers vary with respect to the ages of the children who were observed to be using this strategy. Adam began using it when he was three years, seven months old. He continued using the strategy for only a month or two. Ferreiro and Teberosky (1982), on the other hand, give examples of the strategy being used by two five-year-olds. Genishi and Dyson (1984) do not give the exact ages of the two girls whom they saw use this strategy, but they note that it was used prior to the time that the children began to request spellings from adults, which they did when they were five. Glenda Bissex, the author of a case study of her son Paul (*GNYS AT WORK*, 1980), mentions that Paul used this strategy before she began to keep notes for her book. The first sample she includes in the book was created when Paul was just over five years of age. Therefore, we might assume that Paul used a visual-rule strategy sometime when he was four years old. Most of the children I have observed in the Boston University Preschool use this strategy when they are four years old. In fact, this strategy is the most common one used by children when they are four years old.

It appears, then, that Adam began using this strategy earlier than most other children begin using it and perhaps used it for a shorter period of time than is typical. Perhaps his constant exposure to other children's names in family day-care and nursery school provided him with the information necessary to construct the rules at such an early age.

His relatively brief use of the strategy might have been due to the fact that most of his exploration took place with the magnetic letters on the refrigerator door, in my presence. His exploration was always accompanied by questions about the strings he created. Unlike other children, who create words in a more playful fashion, without seeking feedback, Adam always asked what word he had created or, later, if he had created a word. At nursery school, Adam rarely did any writing. He engaged in play that was more active and social. He wrote at home. In contrast, many of the children—especially girls—in the Boston University Preschool do considerable writing while at school. Their writing is quite social ("Let's make books, okay?" "I'm making a grocery list") and is often shared with peers, not with a teacher.

Different social contexts surely must have different consequences for writing development. For example, when with peers, a child who is creating mock words might announce, "I'm going shopping. I'm getting milk, ice cream, and chocolate chip cookies." Children probably rarely show their lists of mock words to a peer and ask, "What words are these?" Yet, when in the company of an adult, this is likely to be a common question. Because of the different feedback elicited in the two types of social contexts, it wouldn't be surprising if children who spend less time writing among peers and more time writing in the company of adults end up using the visual-rule strategy for a relatively short period of time. I suspect this is what occurred in Adam's case.

Other Children Ask for Spellings

In the last section, we saw that two children observed by Genishi and Dyson (1984) apparently began to ask for spellings after they had experimented with mock words. This strategy has been observed by many other researchers, including Durkin (1966), Hall et al. (1976), and Wells (1986). However, it is difficult to determine, from the general descriptions provided by these authors, when the children asked for spellings or just what questions they asked.

Adam requested spellings at three different times during his writing development. Each time, his questions were unique. His first spelling questions began immediately after he stopped using a visual-rule strategy. During this time, he asked for the spelling of whole words. He rarely attempted a spelling on his own. When he did, it was one that he knew by sight. Sight words included his name and the words "mom," "dad," and "I."

The second time Adam asked spelling questions coincided with the onset of his first phonemic-based spellings. Though he was generating spellings on his own, he often asked for the spellings of individual sounds. At first, when I was unsure how to respond when the situation was ambiguous, I asked him to tell me what word he was trying to spell. When I did this, he let me know that it was a sound, not a word, that he had asked me to spell.

Adam's third period of spelling questions followed a fairly long period of independent (invented) spelling. During this period, he sometimes spelled a word by himself and then asked if it was correct. At other times, he spelled parts of a word by himself and then requested help with the spelling of one specific sound. At other times, he requested the spelling of entire words. His questions during this period were quite selective; he knew when he needed help and what kind of help he needed.

Glenda Bissex (1980) provides enough details in her report of Paul that it is possible to compare his spelling behavior to Adam's. With the exception of the very first period of Adam's spelling requests, which occurred prior to the period covered by Bissex's study, Paul's behavior resembles Adam's quite closely. Bissex says that Paul asked for the spelling of sounds during his early independent spelling period. She suggests that at this point Paul "was not after correctness but rather phonemic transcription—finding some way of representing for himself the significant sounds he distinguished in words" (p. 18). This is exactly what Adam seemed to be after during this phase.

Later, Paul began to ask if a spelling he had generated was right and to ask, as well, for the spelling of entire words. Bissex also noted that it was at this point that Paul's enthusiasm for writing began to wane (p. 4). In fact, she reported that Paul did very little writing between the ages of five years, ten months and six years, three months, almost exactly the same time that Adam went into a writing slump.

Bissex attributed Paul's reluctance to write during this time to the instruction he received in his first-grade classroom. Paul's teacher made children copy correct spellings from adult models (p. 43). Although Adam's classroom had no instruction of this kind, his sound-based spelling strategy also began to suffer from visual interference. Adam, like Paul, had begun to use a conventional, print-governed strategy to read books not long before becoming reluctant to spell. I think reading was the experience that provided the visual knowledge about words that began to make Adam question his own sound-based spellings.

Catherine Snow (1983) also discusses children's reluctance to spell on their own. In reporting about her son, Nathaniel, she said:

. . .though Nathaniel at 4 years could be forced to provide his own spellings, he preferred to copy or be told how to spell things and asked after each letter in a spontaneously spelled word if it were correct. Part of his unwillingness to do spontaneous spelling derived from his knowledge of the arbitrariness of English spelling—he knew that he could not be sure, for example, if a C or an S spelled an /s/, or if C or K was needed for /k/ or if EA, EE, or IE was appropriate for /i/. (p. 184)

According to his mother (Bissex 1980), Paul, too, was aware that one sound could be coded in a variety of ways. She said that she "often asked him what word the sound was in before giving an answer" and did "not know whether my implication that spelling depended on the word context and not just on the isolated sound perpetuated his dependence on adult help in spelling during the first two months he was writing" (p. 19).

As I explained before, I had not complicated Adam's notions about spelling by continuing to ask for the word context, nor did I attempt to explain that some sounds can be coded in more than one way. Adam had "scolded" me for not listening to his questions when I had asked what word he was trying to spell. After that, I was more intent on reassuring him that I was listening than I was on making sure that he realized spelling is complex. After all, I sometimes scolded him for not listening when I asked questions, and I wanted to be sure that I set a good example. Furthermore, given Adam's previous isolated bursts of invented spelling and the long dry spells in between, I wanted to try to get him going independently this time, given his new start. Perhaps my reluctance to introduce complications at this point is what caused Adam to slip rather quickly into a totally independent spelling phase after going through a fairly brief stage of asking for individual sounds.

Catherine Snow's son, Nathaniel, appears never to have gone through an early, independent, naive spelling phase, perhaps because his mother supplied information about the ambiguities of the spelling system right from the start. Paul apparently did go through an independent phase after first going through a fairly protracted period of asking for individual sounds.

The point at which a child begins to read conventionally might dictate his or her approach to spelling. Beginning to read with a print-governed strategy seemed to be related to a new reluctance to spell in both Paul and Adam. And all six of the early readers whom I have observed in the Boston University nursery school over the past five years have been reluctant to spell on their own. I suspect that their visual knowledge was too great to allow their sound-based spellings to stand.

It appears, then, that asking for spellings is a rather common behavior among young children. The course of this behavior may vary among children depending on, among other things, the age at which they begin to read with a print-governed strategy and the way that their spelling questions are answered.

Other Children Create Their Own Phonemic-Based Spellings

Charles Read's book *Children's Categorization of Speech Sounds in English* was published in 1975. This was the first thorough documentation of what has come to be known as "invented spelling." Read demonstrated that children's early spellings are systematic and rule-governed. Among other things, he showed that children use a letter-name strategy in their earliest spellings and that lax vowels often are represented first by the tense vowel whose phonetic features resemble them the most. Additional documentation of Read's findings has been reported since 1975 (Bissex 1980; Henderson and Beers 1980; Gentry 1981, 1982), making invented spelling perhaps the best known of children's emergent literacy behaviors.

What has been reported only infrequently, however, is that some children resist inventing their own spellings. While invented spelling does seem to emerge naturally in many—even most—children, it does not when children (1) are given a lot of information about the complexities of the English writing system when they ask their first spelling questions, and (2) when they begin to read at an early age. In either of these situations, children are likely to be dissatisfied with their invented spellings. There is no evidence, as far as I know, that children's literacy development will suffer if they should show such reluctance during the course of their writing development. In fact, children whose literacy development is the most advanced might be expected to show the most reluctance when asked to invent their own spellings.

This is not to say that invented spelling is harmful to children who do it or that it serves no useful purpose. Quite the contrary! For Adam, as well as for many other children, invented spelling provided an opportunity for independent writing when no other avenue was open. It also allowed Adam to consolidate the letter-sound information he had acquired. Because his father and I responded with information when he asked questions about how specific sounds are represented, Adam acquired additional information about phonetic transcription, which he might otherwise have had little opportunity to acquire in any meaningful way. But invented spelling does run its course. There comes a time when every child becomes too wise to engage in it with naive abandon. Then other measures, such as word banks, word lists, dictionaries, and the like need to be employed.

Some children probably can safely circumvent the use of invented spelling altogether without suffering any undue harm. I think we need not worry that their unwillingness to take risks, as some writers put it (Gentry 1981, 1982; Genishi and Dyson 1984), indicates any great psychological problem. That would be tantamount to suggesting that a five-year-old who knows better than to run into the street after a ball is more reluctant than a two-year-old to take risks. In fact, the five-year-old simply isn't as ignorant as the two-year-old. This is how it seems to me to be with many reluctant, versus enthusiastic, inventive spellers: The inventive spellers are not taking risks; they think they are spelling words *right*. The reluctant child knows more, and digs in his heels.

Many children enjoy a honeymoon with invented spelling because they don't know their spellings are incorrect. Both Adam and Paul enjoyed a period of independent spelling, as we have seen. But then the honeymoon ends, as it did for both Adam and Paul, when children's visual knowledge about words collides head-on with the results of their sound-based spelling system.

Nathaniel, in contrast to Adam and Paul, seemed to have been reluctant to invent spellings from the very start, apparently because he knew too much about the complexities of determining which letter should represent a sound. He, like the four-year-old readers I have observed, always thought invented spelling was a bad idea. When left on their own, without human or other resources to consult, these children create spellings that resemble the inventive spellings of other children, although the spellings of these reluctant children are more conventional. As far as I can determine, however, there is no evidence that there is any advantage to forcing children to create their own spellings when they don't wish to do so. In fact, responding to their reluctance with necessary information might be the best way to help them become independent.

Summary

My purpose in this chapter was to document similarities between Adam's writing development and the writing development of other children. I did not need to dig for days in the library, tracking down obscure references, to find reports of behavior that was similar to Adam's. The examples were there in abundance. Without a doubt, there are other children whose literacy development resembles Adam's.

But not all children develop in exactly the same way. Amidst the similarities, some interesting differences were apparent. In a few cases, there were specific differences in behavior, or at least differences in the way various researchers defined and categorized behavior. The most consistent difference, however, was not found in the behaviors themselves, but in the timing of their emergence.

When one begins to account for differences in development, one enters the realm of theory. Theory goes beyond the documentation of behavior and its variations to probe other questions: What accounts for the emergence of behavior? What conditions make literacy development possible? Why do some children move more quickly or more slowly than others along a developmental path? What causes one child's path of development to diverge a bit from the path of another child? These questions are explored in the next chapter: "Theory Connections."

7 Theory Connections

In this chapter, I first discuss the three major theories of child development, each of which provides a unique explanation of *why* development occurs—what causes a child to move from one level of literacy understanding to another. Then I select the theory that I think best explains Adam's literacy development and discuss changes in his behavior in terms of this theoretical framework.

The Three Major Child Development Theories

Changes in an individual child's behavior and differences in the behavior of different children have been explained in three major ways by child devel-opment theorists. If we think about a continuum of explanations, we have at one end a focus on experi-ence or the environment. In this view, little credit (or blame) is given to inheritance—to the child's genetic endowment. Those who adhere to this view are known as *behaviorists*.

At the opposite end of the continuum are theorists who think that few changes or differences in behavior can be attributed to environment. Internal factors—the child's genetic inheritance—are thought to be the most important determinants of child behavior. Theorists of this persuasion are re-ferred to as *nativists* or *genetic maturationists*.

Between these extremes is the interactional view, or what often is referred to as *cognitive-developmental theory*. In this view, external stimuli are assumed to exert little of the power over behavior that the behaviorist attributes to them, because the child's current level of understanding is thought to moderate their effects. Stimuli, or experiences, have an effect, to be sure, according to cognitive developmentalists, but not in the direct way that a behaviorist assumes. The child's head literally comes between the experience and its effect on the child. It's the modulation of the effect of experience by the child's current level of understanding that leads cognitive developmentalists to claim that development—changes in understanding and behavior—depends on the interaction between the child and his or her experience.

What Causes Changes in Development? Each theory favors a specific explanation for changes in behavior. Behaviorists talk about the importance of breaking learning down into parts and then sequencing these from simple to complex. They talk about eliminating errors, about not moving on to a new skill until an old skill has been mastered. They talk about building up knowledge piece by piece. And they talk about external motivators—reinforcement and punishment. They talk about learning, not about development, because development seems to suggest something that comes from within the child rather than something that gets into the child from the outside.

Genetic maturationists talk about different things. They talk about development and readiness. They talk about waiting until children are ready before attempting to teach them something. They talk about norms and stages and developmental milestones, which they assume emerge in accordance with neurological development that is controlled by the child's genetic endowment.

Cognitive developmentalists, or interactionists, talk about accommodation and assimilation and about equilibration, which is another way of saying that the child tries to resolve contradictions in his or her current way of seeing the world. New experience is assimilated into old mental structures. When it doesn't quite fit, a contradiction—disequilibrium—is created. Accommodation—changes in the current mental structure—then establishes equilibrium, but on a new level of understanding (Piaget 1963).

But according to cognitive developmentalists, accommodation can occur only when the new experience is within the child's *zone of proximal development* (Vygotsky 1978). In other words, if the new experience is totally new, it can't be assimilated into a child's current structure. In this case, no accommodation can result, because there can be no accommodation without assimilation. There also will be no accommodation if no new experience is introduced. If experiences match a child's current mental structures exactly, then nothing new is assimilated, and there will be no change—no accommodation.

According to cognitive developmentalists, motivation has its source in the organism's preference for dissonance at a moderate level. In other words, part of the organism's biological makeup is assumed to involve a preference for new experience that provides for moderate dissonance and manageable accommodation. If experience provides very little that is new, a child would become bored. (What is "moderate" and "manageable" is likely to differ from child to child, depending on such things as the child's genetic endowment and previous history of experience.) If experience provides only what is very novel — experiences for which the child has no current mental structures — then the child would become anxious or frustrated.

The Child Versus Experience in Genetic-Maturational and Cognitive-Developmental Theory Although both genetic-maturational and cognitive-developmental theory give more credit to the child than does behavioral theory, their views about the child's exact role in development differ markedly. Genetic-maturational theory gives almost total credit for development to the child. Structures unfold according to genetically determined timetables. Specific knowledge structures are built into the nervous system, although children still need to learn a specific language or a specific way to deal formally with such things as numbers. But the basic ability to learn a grammar or to learn mathematics is thought to be a matter of innate "wiring." For example, McNeill (1966) proposed a "Language Acquisition Device" as a metaphor for the neurological capability to learn a grammar.

To the cognitive developmentalist, no specific wiring of this kind is assumed. The biological givens are processes, not specific structures. The processes include accommodation, assimilation, and equilibration, along with a built-in tendency to prefer moderate dissonance, which drives the organism to seek experiences that can be assimilated with relative ease.

Experience is less important in genetic-maturational theory than in cognitive-developmental theory. In the former, it is assumed that what's inside will unfold with maturation no matter what the specific experience, as long as the child isn't living in extremely deprived circumstances. In cognitive-developmental theory, structures don't unfold; they must be constructed by the child. This can't occur without experiences that provide for optimal levels of assimilation and accommodation. Even though the cognitive developmentalist assumes a mentally active child who constructs knowledge, experience is absolutely vital. In fact, experience is as important in cognitive-developmental theory as it is in behavioral theory, although the two theories make very different assumptions about how experience affects development. To the behaviorist, experience provides ready-made knowledge and its structure. To a cognitive developmentalist, experience provides opportunities for the child to act mentally to construct and structure knowledge.

Cognitive-Developmental Theory and Adam's Literacy Development

The cognitive-developmental theory appears to provide the best explanation of Adam's literacy development. To make this case, I will first discuss the origin and demise of each of his major ideas about how words should be created. This discussion highlights the experiences from which Adam was able to construct each new idea, as well as the experiences that provided the conflict necessary for him to discard it and move on to a new idea, and, thus, suggests strongly that the ideas did not emerge simply as a matter of maturation. Second, I will discuss the creative (non-imitative) nature of Adam's knowledge constructions. This discussion provides evidence for a cognitive-developmental versus a behavioral view of the role that experience plays in development.

Experiences Related to the Origin and Demise of Adam's Ideas

Specific experiences preceded the origin and demise of each of Adam's word-creation ideas. The timing of these experiences with respect to the development of Adam's ideas suggests that experience rather than maturation might account best for Adam's literacy development.

The Origin and Demise of the Physical-Relationship Hypothesis At first, as we have seen, Adam thought that words should resemble the actual objects or person they were used to represent. His "I'm two, so I need two marks" idea typifies this notion. This idea, I think, had two sources: one conceptual, the other empirical. From his early experiences with paper and pencil, Adam discovered the notion of representation—symbolization. (see Appendix A). But the symbols were concrete—pictures. This picturelike notion of symbolization was the conceptual idea that Adam took to his word-making. At the time, he had no other information about the nature of written symbols.

But in addition to a basic concept about the nature of symbols, Adam needed a specific idea about which characteristics of objects or people to capture in his writing. He latched onto the idea of a quantitative relationship, one in which the length of a word—in this case, a person's name—would match the "size" of the person—the person's age. This kind of relationship between person and word probably occurred to Adam because matching things by size is very common in a young child's experience.

A parent says that these shoes are yours, not your father's, because they are the smaller ones. It's the same with just about everything, including the size of the chair you sit in, the portions of food you are served, and the amount of money you are given to spend. It's no wonder that a child would decide to differentiate between names by maintaining a relationship between their size and the size of their referent.

But what might have made Adam's idea about the symbolic nature of written language change? Conflicting information, I would suggest. In Adam's day-care setting, the children drew and painted quite a lot. The day-care provider always wrote the children's names on their papers simply to keep track of whose paper was whose. One of Adam's best friends was a three-year-old named Elizabeth. Adam must have wondered why her name was so long while his was so short, given that she was but one year older. And why would another two-year-old, named Mike, have a name with four letters, rather than two? Evidence contradicting Adam's physical-relationship hypothesis surrounded him. He couldn't have held onto it for long.

But why did Adam use this hypothesis so early compared to other children cited in the literature? His early family day-care experience might have played a role. In the day-care center he attended during this time, the caregiver was a former art teacher. She was familiar with paint and other art materials and thought these were appropriate for even very young children to use. I think she was probably unique in the extent to which she made art materials available to the children—they could paint and draw every day. Of course, once pictures are made, they have to be labeled with names. This, then, provided an opportunity for Adam to observe written language on a daily basis. Furthermore, given that the words were names of the other children in day care, he knew something about their referents—for example, how old they were. Had he been at home, where pictures do not need to be labeled with names, or in another day-care setting, where the caregiver thought paints and crayons were too messy for two- and three-year-olds, I doubt that he would have given up this first hypothesis about word-making so quickly.

It is also interesting to note that I have never seen a child in the Boston University Preschool use the physical-relationship hypothesis. Children enter at about age three (minimum entry age is two years, nine months). Perhaps the extensive opportunities for drawing and writing in our preschool, and the labeling of drawings with names, propel children quickly past this notion. In addition, we use helper's charts and job charts extensively. These charts provide children with many opportunities to see everyone's name. Finally, given that we have one mixed-age group of three- to five-year-olds, there are frequent discussions about age: "I'm four. How old are you?" As a result, children quickly learn who is three, who is four, and who is five. (They no doubt notice size differences even earlier than they attach ages to other children.) It wouldn't take a particularly observant child in this environment to notice that name length doesn't correlate very well with size or age and that words are arbitrary symbols, not picturelike representations of people.

It also seems reasonable that children could hold onto this early idea for quite a long time if nothing in their experience contradicted it; and it is not hard to imagine environments in which children are given very little experience to contradict it. After all, a child needs to see the word that is used to represent an object or a person and needs to have knowledge about that object or person—whether it's big or little, old or young. I doubt that this information comes together frequently in many young children's environments. Even in many preschools, where painting and drawing are standard parts of the daily experience, teachers often write children's names on children's papers after the child leaves the scene. Because the teacher uses the name as a reference to make sure that the pictures go home with the right child, there seems no reason to have the child write the name (which might be unintelligible to the adult) or to have the child watch as the adult writes it. Nor are charts used routinely for jobs and such in many homes and preschools. It wouldn't be surprising, then, to find that many children who have had extensive preschool experience are still rather naive about the arbitrary nature of written language. It

seems to me that a specific set of events is required to dispel the child's physical-relationship hypothesis about writing and that the child's exposure to that set of events seldom occurs.

The Origin and Demise of the Visual-Design Hypothesis

When Adam's initial idea about word creation was dispelled, he replaced it with an idea that essentially said, "Everybody and everything has a design that stands for it. You have to learn these designs."

This notion could have had its origin in several of Adam's experiences. When a child drew a picture at day-care, for example, his or her name was put on it. The person who wrote the name probably said, "I'll put your name on this picture so we will know that it is yours." Then, when it was time to go home each day, the paintings and drawings were probably scrutinized to see whose was whose. Once again we can imagine the conversation. "Oh, this one is yours. It has your name on it." Or, "This one belongs to Elizabeth. It says 'Elizabeth' right here." Or in the grocery store or when walking down the street, adults might say, "That box says Cheerios," or "That sign says 'Stop'."

When we first tell children what words say, we don't explain in detail. We don't say, "That sign says 'Stop', because it starts with S, which is the letter that says /s/, which is at the beginning when you say the word 'stop'; and then there's a *T*, which is the letter that says /t/ ..." Children are too young to attend to or understand this much information. We simply say, "That sign says ———" or "This is your name with the *A* at the beginning; this is Elizabeth's with the *E*."

This, in any event, is how we talked to Adam. It wasn't surprising, then, that he replaced his first idea with one that assumed written words were very arbitrary symbols. But this idea, too, was short-lived. It was replaced by another idea, one that was less arbitrary, one in which there was at least a link between the oral and written versions of a word.

The Origin and Demise of the Syllabic Hypothesis   Adam could see for himself that he was called "Adam" and that people who read this design on his papers told him that it *said* "Adam." How could he not conclude that the two forms—the oral and the written—were related? But why did he establish a syllabic relationship between the spoken and written forms? Perhaps because syllables are accessible—easy-to-hear—segments of speech (Liberman et al. 1974; Alegria et al. 1982) and because Adam had been exposed to language experiences in which syllables are emphasized.

Mann (1986) has suggested that exposure to poetry and nursery rhymes is enough to make children aware of syllables. Adam was exposed to both, as well as to rhythmic stories and songs, which he often recited. It wasn't much of a leap from hearing language broken up into syllables to breaking it up

that way himself. Then, given the idea that written words should be related to their oral counterparts, it was not much of a step to begin to code syllables heard with one mark each. In Adam's case, the marks used were letters from his name, though they needn't have been.

The demise of the syllabic hypothesis might have come about because of the discrepancy between the length of words Adam created and the words he saw in his environment. Words generated with a syllabic hypothesis tend to be much shorter than the average word. As a result, words Adam created would not have looked like most of the words he was seeing. Furthermore, most of Adam's writing at this point involved his name. Had he written more messages, like those shown in Figure 2—6, the discrepancy between the size of his words and that of the words he saw around him might not have been so obvious. This is because messages contain several words, which, when written down by a young child, are not separated by space. Thus, a multi-word message, if not too long, ends up about as long as many words the child sees. The child's writing and the writing he or she sees would look very similar. But Adam, as noted, wrote mostly his name, and here, particularly given its brevity—two syllables—the discrepancy between his writing and the writing he saw was marked. It is no wonder, I think, that he used the syllabic hypothesis for such a short period of time. Interestingly enough, Adam's next idea was one based on visual rules, on how written words *look*.

The Origin and Demise of the Visual-Rule Hypothesis   Adam saw many words in his environment. At nursery school, which he attended two days a week when he was three years old, there were names on the attendance and helpers' charts, as well as on signs and labels. He also saw his name, and the names of friends, on paintings and charts. Adam also saw words at home. Because his father and I read to him daily, he saw print in books. Even though he focused on the pictures, he sometimes looked at the words in book titles, especially when he told us what book he had selected for us to read. He also addressed greeting cards to "Mommy" and "Daddy." The letters needed to write these words were dictated to him.

Given this access to words, Adam could easily develop some general visual rules for use in generating words. He would have noticed the average length of words, that letters vary within words, and that the same letters appear in many different words, although in a different order. These were the rules that he used to write words that he at first thought were real.

Adam received direct feedback when he used his new visual-rule strategy, because he always asked someone, "What word is that?" I answered this question by sounding out the letter strings he had created. Of course, more often than not the letter string did not turn out to be a real word. Occasion-

ally, I rearranged one of Adam's words, or rearranged the letters, to make a real word. Sometimes, I also arranged the letters on the refrigerator door to make real words, which I left for Adam to find. This was a game we sometimes played.

Perhaps it occurred to Adam during all of this interaction that his visual-rule strategy was not very productive. Other people clearly knew if his strings did or did not form real words. Why not change the strategy to one in which you ask people to write real words for you to copy? Or, when wanting to write a specific message, why not simply ask adults for the spellings you need? I think this is what Adam might have been thinking as he gave up his visual-rule strategy for an authority-based strategy. This strategy, too, was based on the assumption that spelling is essentially a visual task. That hadn't changed. Only the strategy for generating specific words had changed. Then, in the course of obtaining spellings from an adult, another idea emerged.

The Origin and Demise of Adam's Naive Independent Spelling   Once Adam started to use an authority-based strategy, still more information became available to him. At first, I dictated the letters required to spell a word he requested without making explicit the basis for my selections. It seemed enough for him simply to cope with writing the letters down. Later, I began to emphasize the sounds in the word I was spelling before I named the letter needed. Later still, I began to ask Adam what letter *he* thought might come at, for example, the beginning of the word or at the end. With experience of this kind, Adam was able to learn to segment words phonemically and to accumulate knowledge about specific letter-sound associations. Once he was able to segment words phonemically and had some rudimentary letter-sound knowledge, he could begin to generate spellings on his own using a sound-based system. Except for asking for the spellings of specific sounds (versus whole words), he eventually stopped asking for spellings and began to spell independently.

Adam's new, independent spelling strategy worked well for several months, until he began to look more closely at print in books. It was then that he began to notice, again, that his words did not look quite right. This is how his naive independent spelling spree came to an end and how yet another idea was born.

The Origin of Adam's Integrated View of Spelling   Adam's idea that spellings are generated by both sight and sound had several sources. One source was his print-governed approach to storybook reading. (See Sulzby 1985 for a discussion of picture-governed versus print-governed reading strategies.) Adam had not approached books with a print-governed reading strategy prior to the age of five and a half, except for a very brief period prior to his third birthday. I think Adam hadn't tried earlier to read the print in books despite extensive storybook reading experience because he preferred long books, particularly information-rich, nonfiction books. Adam often rejected my suggestion that we read a simple predictable book and picked out a book about dinosaurs, baseball, spaceships, the human body, or soccer. He also liked fairy tales, which we read from an anthology, and chapter books. The only exception to his preference for these kinds of books occurred when I brought home a new simple book. Then he would allow a reading or two of it, but that was about all.

As a result of this preference for very long, print-dense books, which Adam had developed by the age of three, I think it never occurred to him to try to read his books. Furthermore, because the books were not predictable, the lure provided when a child already knows exactly what a book says was not there for Adam. Consequently, he always asked us to read to him.

I have seen many preschool children request to hear familiar books read over and over again. Adam did this from the age of about sixteen months up until the age of three, but not much after that. Therefore, when he first attempted to read books, during January of his kindergarten year (at age five and a half), by *looking at the print*, he had little print-governed reading experience to take to the task. (It's probably worth mentioning here that his preschool and kindergarten classrooms didn't include big-print book experiences.)

Adam's first reading strategy was a strict sounding-out, word-barking approach. This isolated phonics strategy was not one that he learned at nursery school or in kindergarten, where not a single phonics-related ditto sheet was used. Nor was there any other type of isolated phonics instruction. Adam might have gotten his idea that reading is strict graphic-phonemic translation from watching "Sesame Street," to which he remained, even at this late date, a loyal fan. But I suspect that the actual source of his first reading strategy was his writing. I think his thinking went something like this: "If I sound words out to spell them, then I should sound words out to read them."

He continued to try to read, off and on, for about a month, always with a print-dense book. He declined suggestions that he try to read books that were simpler and predictable, and he continued to reject these as candidates for our nightly bedtime story-reading sessions. Although I knew that with just a little practice he could be reading quite well, I did not override his choices. I knew that he would learn to read sooner or later. Furthermore, he was not yet old enough for me to feel that it was worth risking the social-emotional role that our bedtime storyreading served. Besides, I knew that his reading selections would do wonders for his vocabulary and concept development, and that these were as vital to long-term success in reading as was knowledge of the graphic-phonemic system.

By February, Adam had stopped trying to read. Then, in May, he stayed with his grandparents in Illinois for a week while I attended a conference. While there, he saw that his first-grade cousin was able to read several books, including *Go, Dog, Go*. When I joined everyone at the end of the week, I complimented his cousin for her ability to read.

"She's not really reading," Adam told me.

"She is too," I told him.

"Not really," he retorted.

I assumed that he was being a spoilsport, given that his cousin could read while he could not. Therefore, rather than ask him to explain himself and tell me why he claimed that his cousin couldn't read, I told him that he was being rude and that I didn't want him to say anything more about it. He didn't.

From that time on, I think Adam looked at print a little differently and tried more often to read it. There was an increase, for example, in his response to signs on highways and storefronts. I think he even looked at the print in some of his simpler storybooks, which were still on his bookshelf, although he always wanted me to read more complicated books for his bedtime story, which I did. Occasionally, I would suggest that we also read some simpler books and that he help me. He continued to reject this idea. Then, one morning in September, before he left for school, he said, "I bet I can read *Go, Dog, Go*. That's really an easy book to read."

There still was a copy on his bookshelf, one he hadn't been interested in since he had memorized it at about age two. I said, "Well, you have a copy of that book. I'll put it out on your bed and we can read it tonight." I located the book and placed it on his bed and then went back to the kitchen to finish up the dishes. In a few minutes, he came into the kitchen with the book in hand. He sat down and read the whole thing. His reading definitely was print-governed. I could tell by its pace and by the adjustments he made in a few words, given the graphics on the page. But he obviously remembered the story, both from our earlier readings of it when he was two and, no doubt, from the more recent exposure provided by his cousin.

He was delighted that he could read the book and also was somewhat surprised. When I said, "See, you can read," I mistook for modesty his response of, "Well, not really; not really very good." It was only later, in November, a good two months after this incident and quite a few books later, that I fully realized what had been going on.

When I picked him up from school one day, he said, "Know what, Mom? I'm really a good reader."

I told him that I knew he was, and that I had known it for a long time. "But you sound surprised," I told him.

"Well," he said, "I didn't used to think I was."

"Why not?"

"Well, because I didn't think that you could *remember* words; I thought you were supposed to sound them all out."

"Why did you think that?" I asked.

"I don't know," he said, with a sort of incredulous expression. "I just did."

I apologized for my attack on his motives during the incident with his cousin the previous May, because now, six months later, I realized that his remark about his cousin's reading ability had been serious. She was fairly fluent and was not sounding out any of the words. Given Adam's concept of reading, this did not count. He didn't think he could read, and he hadn't thought that she could either. (I've yet to figure out how he thought his parents read. We certainly didn't sound words out. Did he think that we just knew what was in those books, or do such glaring contradictions and inconsistencies simply escape a preschooler's mind?)

Thus, Adam was about six years old (specifically, five years, ten months) before he began really to inspect print. Interestingly enough, it was in June, only a few weeks after his stay at his grandparents', that he first refused to write his own story in kindergarten (see Figure 3–16). This was the beginning of his reluctance to write because his words didn't look right. There had been the "kat"/"cat" incident (Figure 3–15) a week or so before he had made the trip to his grandparents, so the conflict between sight and sound could have started prior to his seeing his cousin read.

If writing had presented Adam with a stumbling block during his first attempt to read (during January, at the age of around five and a half), when he tried to sound words out, now it was reading that upset his ability to write. After beginning to pay more attention to the words in books, he found that the words he wrote no longer looked right.

But it would be more experience with writing, this time experience observing me write words in his dictionary at home and explaining how I was doing it, that would provide him with the information he needed to resolve his latest dilemma. It was from this experience that he discovered that words are not always written the way they sound, that there is more to it than that. Soon a question began to follow when he wrote words. It was, "Is that right?"

Although Adam's spellings were far from conventional even several months after he adopted his sound-plus-sight approach, his conceptualization of the spelling process had moved to an entirely different level. He had a lot of spelling details to iron out, to be sure, but never again would there be a revolution in his concept of spelling. He had righted himself for the last time with respect to the demands of English orthography. No major conflict remained between his knowledge about spelling and the spelling system with which he interacted.

Evidence of Active and Creative Knowledge Construction

The preceding section provides considerable evidence in support of an interactional model of development. But before clinging firmly to this conclusion, the data require another test. Is there evidence of active knowledge construction as well? If the role of experience is to provide opportunities for children to construct knowledge, rather than to provide the knowledge or its structure directly, we should be able to find creative knowledge structures that differ from those Adam saw demonstrated. In addition, we should be able to see new, rule-based knowledge override previous knowledge structures, especially in cases where the initial concepts were due only to imitation.

The following discussion presents evidence for a creative aspect to Adam's knowledge creation. The examples presented are not exhaustive. Only a few have been selected for the purpose of illustrating the creative (i.e., novel or self-generated) nature of Adam's learning.

Adam's Syllabic Hypothesis   Adam never saw anyone use the syllabic hypothesis to create words. Had he lived in a different language community, one that uses a syllabary, he would have seen individual marks being used to code syllables. But he was not a member of such a community. Adam's idea seems to have been created by Adam, although it was based on experience. Adam had heard people refer to him by name and had no doubt seen people refer to the printed version of his name. Therefore, he had reason to connect the two versions of his name. But why in this specific way? As explained earlier, Adam had heard songs, rhythmic stories, nursery rhymes, and poems. In these, the emphasis was on syllabic segmentation. As a result, Adam put together the two ideas—that written language codes oral language and that oral language can be broken into syllabic segments. His syllabic hypothesis was born.

Prior to his use of this hypothesis, Adam had written his name using four characters, because he had assumed that each thing, including himself, had a certain design (see, for example, Figure 1–3). But then, given his new idea, and despite what he continued to see, he began to write his name with two characters instead of four (Figure 1–5). The conceptual rule took over in much the same way that it does when children are learning oral language and begin to overgeneralize typical past-tense verb endings to verbs that are irregular (Brown 1973). They start out by saying, "Daddy ran," and "I beat Tommy," but once they develop a general rule with respect to past-tense verb endings, they begin to say, "Daddy runned," and "I beated Tommy."

Children's earliest use of correct information, in instances such as those cited above, is based on imitation, not on knowledge-constructed rules. Rules, general principles or views of the world, are much more powerful, and they bring sweeping changes in their wake. Something picked up through imitation is brushed aside.

Adam's Distinction Between Pictures and Writing There was another case of rule overrun, at three years of age, when Adam made a sharp distinction between pictures and writing. Even though he had used alphabet letters to write his name, he stopped using them for a period of several months after he realized that pictures and writing are different. He excluded the internal features—specific letters—that we require as a criterion to judge writing and focused instead on its overall organization—on its linearity. (See Appendix B.)

Adam certainly had not observed anyone else make this distinction, in this specific way. It was a creative distinction that he made on his own. Before this, he had written his name using alphabet letters. But he stopped using letters for several months, until his idea about what made writing and pictures different had changed.

Adam's Invented Spellings Adam's early, phonemic-based spellings differed markedly from the spellings that others gave him and the ones that he saw in his environment. His emerging sound-based system overpowered what he saw. The changes Adam made in his spelling of the word "love" provide another example. He had requested this word quite often during his authority-based word-creation stage, and of course the conventional spelling was given to him. Yet, when he began to generate his own spellings, he first changed the spelling to "LUV," and then to "LV." It wasn't that he forgot how the word should look; it was that a new, and powerful, rule-based idea overrode his earlier, surface-structure knowledge.

Knowledge Is Constructed   These three examples provide strong evidence for the interactionist theory, with its constructivist claims. Adam, as we have seen, created his own knowledge. He did not passively take in knowledge in the form that was presented to him.

Summary

We can see the clear impact of experience in Adam's literacy development. Without relevant, redundant (i.e., ubiquitous), and appropriate literacy experiences, a child's mind, no matter how active or creative, cannot construct appropriate notions about written language. But it is also true that no matter how simple or efficient it might seem merely to transfer what we know, ready-made, from our heads into the heads of children, we find inevitably that their minds keep getting in our way. This fact does not diminish the importance of the adult's role in a child's education. There is a large and extremely important role for adults to play. And if they don't play it, children's literacy development will suffer—terribly. But we can't do the learning for children and try simply to stuff it into their heads. Children must do the learning. Our job is to keep them in situations where they can learn the things we consider important and to scaffold—provide support for—their interactions when tasks are beyond the capacity of their own independent behavior.

CHAPTER

8

Teaching Connections

There were many moments while working on this book that I thought about its implications for teaching. In hindsight, I often could see how I might have been more helpful to Adam. There were times, too, when I thought that Adam's teachers might have been more helpful. But to be effective, teachers need considerable knowledge about literacy development. Despite my own seven or eight years of experience in the area of early literacy development prior to Adam's arrival, I lacked a coherent framework for thinking about a child's progress. Without such a framework, it was difficult to know what Adam was doing and to facilitate his learning effectively.

I was clearer about theory, about the relative impact of maturation versus experience on development, given my educational background and strong interest in child development. I have leaned toward cognitive-developmental theory since I read Joe McVicker Hunt's book, *Intelligence and Experience* (1965), more than twenty years ago. Nothing appearing in the research literature since then has caused me to change my mind. In fact, across almost all domains of development, an interactionist or cognitive-developmental perspective seems to account best for optimal child outcomes.

Clarity about theory, more than specific knowledge about literacy development, was what enabled me to do something appropriate in relation to Adam most of the time. Even if I didn't know exactly what was going on at a specific time, I continued to think that experience and adult interaction and involvement in a child's learning were important. With this general stance, I usually figured out, sooner or later (often later rather than sooner), some way to be helpful. By staying involved, by continuing to provide experiences, and by trying to pay attention to what a child does, it is possible to learn from a child and to correct one's course of action. This is a somewhat sloppy way to teach, to be sure, but it's difficult to proceed in any other way when the knowledge base necessary to understand the course of development in a particular area is patchy. Luckily, children continue to put up with us, as long as we keep trying and come through part of the time.

In this chapter, I discuss the impact that knowledge about children and knowledge about theories of development have on teaching.

Using Knowledge About Development to Guide Teaching

A few years ago, while giving a lecture to a group of kindergarten teachers, I discussed the methods we use to promote literacy development in the Boston University Preschool. I mentioned that we often spell words for children who ask for them and that we also provide frequently requested words on word rings in the classroom writing/drawing center. After the lecture, there was a somewhat heated debate about whether young children should be given spellings or whether they should be made to create

their own. I advocated the assistance approach, while most of the audience claimed that the independence model was better. According to these teachers, assistance would inhibit the development of children's own spelling strategies.

On the way home from the lecture, I almost decided that we should test the approach suggested by these teachers. As the director of a laboratory preschool where many student interns are trained, I was all too familiar with preschoolers' skill in getting adults to do for them many of the things that they actually can do for themselves. I wondered if their getting us to give them spellings was another instance of the same phenomenon. But I decided that it wasn't, that in this case the children needed the spelling assistance they requested. (To clarify, the issue with such young children was not whether they can generate correct spellings independently; of course they cannot. I wasn't any more concerned about correctness in spelling for such young children than were the kindergarten teachers. The disagreement was about *when* children are able to generate even these first phonemic-based spellings and about what role the adult plays in launching children into this sort of behavior.)

We Didn't Know
What We Were Talking About

Later, after developing the overall framework for word-creation strategies described earlier in this book, I understood better the kindergarten teachers' concerns. For the most part, they worked with children who lived in circumstances that would have afforded them extensive literacy experiences during their preschool years. Most of these children probably entered kindergarten already able to segment words phonemically. They probably also knew many letter-sound correspondences. But even with this knowledge, children can continue to ask for spellings instead of creating their own. Often, a nudge toward independence is required, and perhaps this is what the teachers in my audience had experienced.

However, the younger children with whom I had worked and to whom I had been giving spellings had only recently given up a visual-rule word-creation strategy for an authority-based one. They almost never had more than a beginning ability to segment words phonemically, and few knew many letter-sound associations. Most children don't have these abilities as three-year-olds, or even as young four-year-olds. Most preschoolers code words syllabically or they create strings of letters ("mock" words), selecting and arranging them according to visual rules. They don't ask for spellings while they use these hypotheses. Only after they give up these strategies and begin to utilize an authority-based strategy do they begin to ask for spellings. Then, when adults who give these make phonemic segmentation and the systematic use of letter-sound associations explicit, children begin again to write independently. This time, their spellings are phonemic-based and readable.

By the time children have had enough experience with written language to reach this level, they typically are leaving preschool and entering kindergarten. It's the unusual preschooler, in my experience, who begins to create words in this way much before four or four and a half years of age. But many of the preschoolers who leave our program at Boston University, usually around the age of five or five and a half, are either creating spellings on their own or are on the verge of figuring out how to do so.

In fact, when I looked more closely at teacher behavior in our mixed-age group of three- to five-year-olds, I noticed a variety of responses to children's spelling questions. For example, some of the older children who had been asking for spellings of whole words for several months often were asked to help the teacher generate a requested spelling. Sometimes the teacher pronounced the word slowly, as if she had to think about it herself. The child was included in this thinking process by the glance of the teacher and by her puzzled facial expression, which seemed to say, "What letter would we need to start this word?" Sometimes children were asked outright, "What do you think?" or "How do you think we should spell that word?" In these cases, there was no sounding out, thinking-out-loud display. Instead, the child was expected to do even that part for him- or herself. In other words, teachers began to up the ante when they thought that children were ready. But at first they stayed involved to provide a display of the segmenting process the child would need to employ. Later, the entire process was thrown back to the child, although the teachers stood ready to intervene when they saw that the child couldn't move ahead alone. In other words, had my reference group been our older preschool children one year later, during their kindergarten year, I probably would have agreed much more with the strategies being proposed by the teachers who attended my lecture.

As it turned out, both the kindergarten teachers and I probably were right in our claims about the appropriateness of our strategies for most of the children who served as our reference groups. But with our "mindless methodology" mentalities, neither they nor I knew that we were talking about children who were, as groups, at remarkably different developmental levels. As a result, our conversation focused on the uses of specific methodologies without a framework for discussing them sensibly.

The Dangers Involved in Trial-and-Error Teaching

A trial-and-error approach to the selection of teaching methods has some very high costs. New teachers often take several years to discover methods that are effective with most children they teach. In the meantime, many children can suffer. Teachers who move from one school to another can misapply in the new situation what worked for them in the old one. More children can suffer. Teachers who hit upon something that works for most children can view the few children for whom it doesn't work as problems, when no problems actually exist. A few more children suffer. (See Appendix C for a case study of a child who suffered because her literacy development was more advanced than her kindergarten peers.) "Experts" who give lectures can advocate methods without specifying the contexts within which they are most likely to be useful. Still more children can suffer.

We need to do better than this. But we need comprehensive conceptions of children's literacy development to guide us. Without these, we cannot help but latch onto specific procedures—methods— and then apply these inappropriately to all children, whether they work or not. Sometimes, parents can work at home to correct our errors. At other times, children probably simply lose out.

But in addition to specific information about development, teaching is also influenced by theoretical assumptions.

Theory and Teaching: An Illustration of Their Connection

Our theories—our basic assumptions about development—influence how we behave with children. In fact, only when certain assumptions are made about the nature of development does it make sense for teachers to select carefully the teaching strategies they use with individual children. In the following discussion we see how the same set of circumstances can be interpreted and responded to differently by two different teachers, given their theoretical assumptions.

A Genetic-Maturational Approach to Events   In a recent issue of *Reading Today*, a column described a kindergarten teacher who had become frustrated with her children's dependence on adults for spellings during classroom story-writing periods (Wood 1989). Prior to the period in which the teacher had started to try to support the children's independent writing, the teacher apparently had assumed that young children were incapable of writing and had written for them (i.e., had taken dictation). However, the teacher was disappointed and frustrated to find that acceptance of children's invented spellings did not result in writing that adults could read. Only when adults helped children sound out words and record what they heard could all children produce phonemic-based spellings that adults could actually read. This was of concern to the teacher, because she typically read the children's stories to the class.

Upon the advice of another kindergarten teacher, this teacher decided to change her tactics. Instead of expecting children to perform at the level required to produce phonemic-based invented spellings, she decided to allow the children to use whatever form of "writing" they wanted to use. She also decided to rely on the children to read their own stories; no longer would an adult read them.

To introduce children to the new system, she showed drawings, scribblings, strings of letters, invented spellings, and conventional spellings. She explained that children could use whichever of these strategies they wanted to use. Furthermore, they were told that they would need to write on their own, without teacher help. The teachers, she explained, would be doing some writing of their own and would not be available to help children spell words.

On the first day after the discussion and demonstration, children continued to ask for spellings. But the teacher and her aides did not answer their questions. Children were reminded about the forms of "writing" they could use and were told that the teachers were too busy with their own writing to help them.

According to the author, "By the end of several days, during which the teachers reviewed writing forms and steadfastly remained too busy to help children 'spell,' virtually all of the children were writing independently, using a variety of forms of emergent writing. The children showed true enjoyment of the process and 'read' their productions easily, with text-reading intonations and language. Writing in the kindergarten had changed dramatically" (p. 22). The author reports that many children began to draw as a way to write. The author concludes, "When teachers' expectations are aligned with developmentally appropriate behaviors, they encourage and accept emergent writing in all of its forms, and the children become motivated, eager writers" (p. 22).

This report describes a teacher who seems to have changed from a behaviorist to a genetic maturationist. After despairing of her attempts to teach all the children the same high-level word-creation strategy (phonemic-based spelling), she decided to leave all the children alone. Apparently, she felt that they would develop according to their own individual timetables. The teacher saw no role for herself in the children's literacy development, except that she provided materials for writing and asked children to write. This is the equivalent of a gardener who provides water, fertilizer, and sunshine for plants. A genetic maturationist views children in very much the same way. Meddling or intervening gets in the way. The preferred approach is to provide an appropriate environment and then leave children alone to grow.

How a Teacher with Cognitive-Developmental Views Might Have Responded to the Same Events

A teacher operating within a cognitive-developmental framework probably would have responded differently to the situation described above. She, too, would have given up trying to use the same strategy to get all of the children to write in the same way. She would believe that different children are at different levels of understanding at any given time, and the processes of assimilation and accommodation require that a teacher match teaching strategies to a child's current level of development. Therefore, rather than giving up and withdrawing from the situation altogether to let children develop on their own, a cognitive-developmental teacher would try to find out each child's level of understanding and then adapt her interactions to each child's level of development. Such a teacher would make sure that the classroom writing center provides for a number of writing possibilities, ranging from play with writing to functional writing to story writing.

A cognitive-developmental teacher would probably not give a story-writing assignment to all of the children. She would know that, for example, a child who is creating words by stringing letters together (that is, one who is using a visual-rule theory of word construction) might profit little from story-writing assignments, because stories require the child to attribute meaning to the writing created. As long as the child is asked to "tell us what your story says," the child is led to believe that writers can attribute their own meaning to print. If not given specific assignments to write stories, however, children often play at word creation and then take their creations to adults to ask, "What word is this?" This situation is the one in which the child receives useful feedback—that not all letter strings yield actual words. This information is what seems to introduce the essential cognitive dissonance or conflict, which then prompts children to stop creating, and attributing meaning to, mock words and to create words instead by asking for spellings. It is in this situation that children can observe demonstrations of phonemic segmentation, as adults think out loud when generating spellings in response to children's questions.

Limiting children's writing to this sort of word play bothers some teachers, who think that children can profit from experience in composing stories. If a teacher feels this way, stories can be generated in other contexts, ones that don't require the child to write the words down. For example, children can talk about their drawings or paintings, and they can engage in dramatic play, a context in which complex stories are sure to be spun. (This teacher does not call drawing "writing," because it isn't. It's a form of communication, to be sure, but it is not writing. Writing is a different form of communication, one that follows very different rules.) Or teachers can ask children to record their stories on audiotape.

A child who has just begun to move beyond a visual-rule strategy for creating words will ask for spellings. From a cognitive-developmental perspective, spellings would need to be given at first, if the child is to be able to develop the understanding required to become independent in spelling. The strategy of thinking out loud—of sounding words out and naming letters used to code them—is probably a useful one to use with children just beginning to use this strategy. As time goes on, children can be asked to participate more fully both in segmenting words and in selecting letters to code what they hear. Interactions of this sort provide the experience needed for the child to develop the ability to segment words phonemically and to realize that alphabet letters are used systematically to represent specific sounds. It also allows children to learn some specific letter-sound correspondences, or at least to realize that their knowledge of letter names can be exploited for a specific purpose.

But it's unlikely that all children who ask for spellings are at this critical juncture. Others probably can segment words phonemically and can code what they hear somewhat systematically with alphabet letters. These children don't need a teacher to make explicit in a thinking-out-loud sort of way how she's creating a spelling. They could be encouraged to move on to segmenting words and coding what they hear without this preliminary experience. But these children still will ask questions about how to code specific sounds. Later, children who have become very independent inventive spellers can profit from additional strategic teaching. Gradually, children need to be made aware of the discrepancy between their own and conventional spellings. From a cognitive-developmental perspective, teachers have a role to play here and can provide opportunities that lead children to notice such variances. For example, teachers can read children's stories or other writing and can write a response using some of the words (spelled conventionally) that the child spelled unconventionally. This increases the chances that children will notice a discrepancy between their spellings and conventional spellings. Once a discrepancy has been noticed, children begin to search for some resolution to the contradiction. Teachers also can publish children's stories, using conventional spellings to replace children's inventions.

Children who are aware of the contradiction between invented and conventional spellings are ready to profit from even more information. Some instruction in basic phonics makes sense at this point, because it helps the child to understand how words can be spelled one way even though they sound another way. A child at this level can be helped to achieve more independence in writing through the use of word lists and personal dictionaries. A child also could be taught to focus on conventional spelling when writing a second draft of a story or when writing a "social" piece, such as a greeting card or a letter. Children can be helped to write efficiently by knowing when to focus on conventional spelling (in a second draft) and when to ignore it (in a first draft). This is quite different from trying to convince children that their spellings are "right for them," which fails to acknowledge the fact that their spellings aren't conventional. Teachers can acknowledge that the spellings aren't conventional but then explain to a child that *in some situations* it isn't necessary to worry about it, while in other situations, it is.

A Summary of the Differences in Teaching Based on Genetic-Maturational and Cognitive-Developmental Views The teachers described above are similar in that they recognize the futility of trying to achieve a certain level of functioning without taking into account what the child brings to the situation. But the genetic maturationist ends up leaving much more to the child than does the cognitive developmentalist. We might say that the cognitive developmentalist is *child*-centered while the genetic maturationist is *children*-centered. This is a very big difference.

I think it would be accurate to say that genetic maturationists don't provide developmentally appropriate instruction, even though they often claim that they do. Developmentally appropriate instruction, it seems to me, is instruction that takes account of where a child is and then provides experiences that move a child on. Teachers who simply allow children to use their current knowledge and skills without any concern for helping them to move to a new level cannot be said to be instructing them at all, although from a genetic-maturational perspective instruction necessarily amounts to staying out of children's way to make it possible for children's natural development to proceed.

Literacy Development and Teaching: Some Final Thoughts

It seems to me that a number of problems need to be solved if teachers are to be truly effective in facilitating children's literacy development. One problem is that we lack rich and complex frameworks for thinking about children's literacy development. Sulzby's (1985) developmental framework for story reading, along with the frameworks provided by Ferreiro and Teberosky (1982) and this study of

Adam, provide virtually the only coherent conceptions of early literacy development currently available. And even these conceptions are limited, given that they deal with small numbers of children living in specific circumstances and so may not apply to all children. This doesn't give teachers much to go on. Future research needs to fill this gap. We need longitudinal studies of many children living in a variety of circumstances. In the meantime, teachers might try to work together, across age and grade levels, to develop frameworks for themselves, perhaps by doing their own case studies and sharing the data with each other.

A second problem, it seems to me, is that teachers tend to conceptualize development in terms of two extremes. They think that they must either teach everything directly—provide ready-made knowledge and knowledge structures—or that they must pull back completely, leaving development entirely to the child. If children progress when teachers follow the second course, the teachers tend to attribute developmental progress to internal factors, not to experience. Teachers often forget that many children have parents who provide considerable instruction, informal though it may be. As a consequence, teachers might be attributing more to maturation than is warranted.

Researchers in the area of early literacy development are not very helpful with respect to this issue. In many studies, developmental changes are reported, but the causes of these changes are not accounted for. Theoretical assumptions are made, however, and too often, the change is assumed to come from within the child.

Marie Clay (1983) offers a suitable and too infrequent caution about this matter. After discussing the developmental changes in children's ideas about how words are created and how conventional spelling works, she has this to say:

What is not clear from the reports at hand is whether the shift in conventional spelling occurs simply as a result of teachers fostering large quantities of writing without their giving specific attention to the factors which encourage these shifts, or whether such additional factors as the reading programme, the questions teachers ask, who reads the child's stories and how they react to these stories, among others, are necessary to bring about the conventionalization of spelling.

I suspect the shifts occur because of active comparisons that the child engages in. The teacher, in interaction with the young writer, has something to do with some of the shifts that occur. I am always wary of statements which imply the naturalness or inevitability of learning something. (p. 263)

Children's learning would benefit considerably, I think, if teachers would stop choosing between theoretical extremes and would stop viewing all instruction, no matter how well adapted and responsive to a child's current level of understanding, as developmentally inappropriate and anti-child. As far as I know, the bulk of research in virtually all areas of development shows *positive* results from *responsive* adult involvement with children and negative results from both intrusive interaction and ignoring or neglect.

But a cognitive-developmental perspective does pose some problems. Perhaps the most important one is that it is extremely labor intensive. It's much easier to teach all children the same thing in the same way or to do the opposite and simply withdraw from the scene, leaving learning and development to the child. In both of these cases the teacher doesn't need to figure out what individual children are thinking or how to adapt instruction to move individual children along. But there are ways to cope with the extra work that interactive teaching requires. Parent or other volunteers can be enlisted to help in the classroom, for example, and parents can be asked to provide information about their child's current behavior and understanding. Parents can also be asked and expected to provide experiences at home. (Yes, some parents won't want to or be able to do it; others will.)

It has been interesting to me as a parent to realize that teachers almost never ask me to tell them what I know about Adam's current behavior or understanding. Even simple questions, such as "Does he ever string letters together and ask you what words he's made?" or "Does he ever comment that his spellings don't look like spellings he sees in books or on signs?" or "How many objects have you seen him count accurately?" were never asked. Teachers give us progress reports, but they rarely ask us for any. As a consequence, a vital source of information and instruction is lost.

I often felt that I knew far more about Adam's understanding than his teachers. This isn't too surprising, given that I was dealing just with him, while his teachers were dealing with twenty or more children at a time. In addition, he gets a new teacher every year, and the process of getting acquainted must start all over again. At this point, I have an eight-year edge on his new teacher for next year.

I don't think I'm a terribly unusual parent. Over and over again, parents of the children in the Boston University Preschool tell us something that their child is doing before we've noticed it. They do this, I think, because we provide frameworks for looking at literacy and number development and then explain these to parents in newsletters or conferences. With these frameworks in hand, parents are put in a position to recognize changes in behavior and to tell us about them. As teachers, we need to exploit this parent resource more fully than we have done in the past. There's enough work to go around when it comes to educating children, and we need to ask parents to do their share.

In short, I think our ability to facilitate children's literacy development can improve if we develop coherent frameworks for thinking about children's development, think more clearly about our theoretical choices and make our teaching more consistent with a cognitive-interactionist perspective, and involve parents more completely as partners in their children's education. It's a tall order, but one that Adam's story compels us to try to fill.

Appendices

Adam's Discovery of the Symbolic Potential of Lines

Chapter 1 begins when Adam created his first word, at the age of two years, eight months. But Adam's experiments with marks began long before this eventful day. Adam was given a pencil and paper for the first time when he was one year old. He had frequent access to paper and writing materials from that time forward, although, prior to the age of three, he did not have free access. The walls and furniture couldn't have stood it!

Throughout the year and a half that preceded his first word-making attempt, Adam discovered some important notions about writing tools and symbolization. First, he discovered that writing tools could make a record of his arm movements. When he was given paper and a pen for the first time, he seemed fascinated by the pen itself. He alternately made a mark and looked carefully at the pen, as if trying to figure out just how all of this was happening.

The sample created during his first session with pen and paper is shown in Figure A–1. The pattern created consists of random marks. Adam didn't inspect the marks after making each one. Instead, he inspected the pen, and then made another mark.

After his fascination with the marking tool itself wore off, Adam began to pay closer attention to the marks themselves. Within six months (at the age of one year, six months), he began deliberately to repeat marks that he had made. For example, in Figure A–2, he made a series of horizontal straight lines as

**Figure A−1   Adam's First Marks
(Age 1 Year)**

**Figure A−2   Repeating Marks
(Age 1 Year, 6 Months)**

well as tight patches of scribble, all of which looked very much alike. He looked closely at his paper when creating this sample, as if he were trying intentionally to recreate the same kind of line several times over.

The sample shown in Figure A–3 marked the first occasion (at the age of one year, seven months) that Adam labeled his markings— said they looked like, or were, something. In this particular case, he said they were "G's." After making the first one, he commented, as if surprised, "A G!" He made a second one and commented, "'Nother G." Others followed, always with the comment, "'Nother one; 'nother one."

It is doubtful that Adam set out to draw G's on his paper. He seemed to create the first one by accident. He noticed that it was similar to G's he'd seen on the rim of his baby dish (he often pointed to the embossed letters and asked, "Dat?"). At this point he labeled it and then seemed intentionally to continue to create more of these forms.

The sample shown in Figure A–4 shows another example of deliberate repetition of certain kinds of lines. This piece looks like a deliberate attempt to contrast vertical and horizontal lines. It was created when Adam was one year, ten months old. On the same day that this sample was created, Adam also

Figure A–3 Adam's *G's* (Age 1 Year, 8 Months)

Figure A–4 More Deliberate Repetition (Age 1 Year, 10 Months)

**Figure A—5 "A Man, Mouth and Eyes"
(Age 1 Year, 10 Months)**

created the drawing shown in Figure A—5. He said it was "a man, mouth and eyes." Again, I doubt that Adam set out to draw a man. I suspect that the lines he put on the paper simply reminded him of a man, with mouth and eyes, so he labeled his drawing accordingly. But clearly, Adam was beginning to get the idea that lines could represent objects and patterns he saw in the world.

A significant shift in Adam's marking behavior occurred at the age of two years, five months, when he seemed to deliberately set out to draw something. Two samples are shown in Figure A—6. He drew the outer curved line of Figure A—6A first, and then placed the three lines within it. He made no comment. Then he drew the sample shown in Figure A—6B. When finished, he said, "I made a big circle and a little circle." It's highly unlikely that he would accidentally have made two marks with such contrasting features. It is more likely that he set out to draw a big circle and a little circle.

Figure A−6   Adam's Drawings (Age 2 Years, 5 Months). A: First Drawing. B: Big Circle and Little Circle.

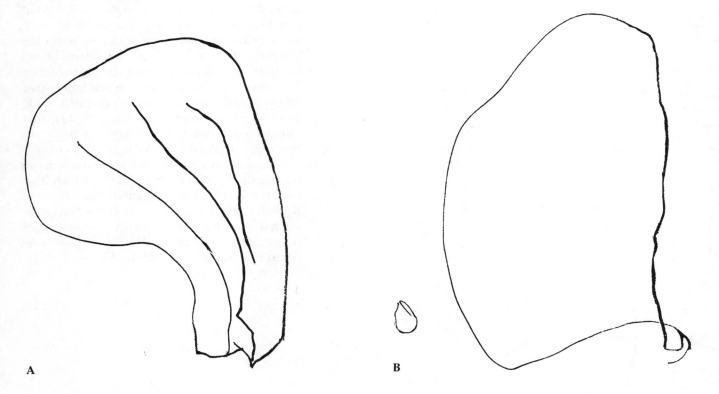

A

B

Figure A−7   First Letters: E, T, H, L (Age 2 Years, 7 Months)

Two months later, Adam asked me about some index cards I had left on the kitchen table. I explained that I use these to write on. He asked for some that he could write on, and I gave some to him. Then he asked, "What can I write?" I suggested that he try to write some of the magnetic letters that were on the refrigerator door. I took several letters (*E*, *T*, *H*, and *L*) down and placed them on the table. He very deliberately and painstakingly tried to copy each of the letters, and even made three *T*'s and two *H*'s, because his first attempts did not suit him (Figure A−7). In this episode, Adam clearly set out to create a particular form before he started to draw. Even his question, "What can I write?", which he'd never asked before, indicated that he was thinking about what he would do before he started to draw. This was the beginning of intentional, pictorial representation. It pre-dated the sample shown in Figure 1−1 by two weeks.

Adam Learns to Distinguish
Pictures and Print

Soon after Adam wrote his name by using three lines (Figure 1–1), he began to write his name using alphabet letters that looked fairly conventional. One of his first attempts, made at the age of two years, nine months, is shown in Figure B–1. Another attempt, this one dictated by the rules of the syllabic hypothesis, is shown in Figure B–2.

During this same period, Adam often drew alphabet letters, literally making a picture of them. In the sample shown in Figure B–3A, *M*'s are drawn; in the sample shown in Figure B–3B, *A*'s are drawn. He also included drawings of alphabet letters in pictures that contained drawings of other things, such as people (see Figure B–4). He was about two years, nine or ten months old at the time Figure B–4 was drawn.

Figure B–1   Adam's Name (Age 2 Years, 9 Months)

141

Figure B–2   Another Attempt to Write Name (Age 2 Years, 10 Months)

Figure B–3   Pictures of Letters. A: *M*'s (Age 2 Years, 10 Months). B: *A*'s (Age 2 Years, 10½ Months).

A

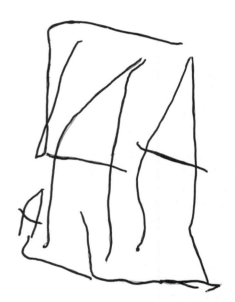

B

Figure B−4 Drawings of Letters and Other Things (Age 2 Years, 9 or 10 Months)

Figure B–5   Scribble Marks (Age 3 Years)

Up to this point, Adam seemed to have differentiated writing and pictures in terms of their overall organization. Writing was lined up, while pictures could be arranged more randomly on the page. The marks or forms— the content—of writing and drawing, however, could be the same.

But by age three, Adam had begun to notice that the internal features, the actual forms of the lines making up writing versus pictures, also varied. At first, Adam stopped including alphabet letter forms in his writing. He substituted small scribble marks, like those shown in the bottom right corner of the sample shown in Figure B–5.

For several months, Adam signed his name in scribble, rather than by writing it out using alphabet letters. An example of his signature at this time is shown in the upper left corner of Figure B–6. Also during this time, Adam filled whole pages with scribble writing and said they were "letters to his dad." One of these is shown in Figure B–7.

Finally, after a period of about five months, Adam began again to write his name and other words using alphabet letters. The first reappearance occurred when he wrote "Daddy" and then his own signature in a birthday card for his father. The word "Daddy," which was written on the envelope to the card, showed a scribble-letter for each letter, except for the D, which did resemble

Figure B−6   Adam's Signature (Age 3 Years)

Figure B−7   Letter to Dad (Age 2 Years, 11 Months)

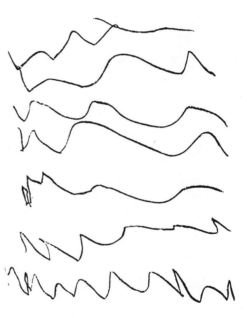

Figure B–8   Using Letters (Age 3 Years, 5 Months). A: "Daddy." B: "Adam S."

A

B

HAPPY BIRTHDAY

an uppercase *D*. Inside, Adam signed his name, A-D-A-M S (see Figure B–8).

It's difficult to know exactly why Adam rejected alphabet letters for this period of several months. Perhaps he rejected them because he had previously drawn pictures of them and thought of them as pictures. Or perhaps he couldn't make his letters look small and regular enough, like the print he saw in books. Whatever his reasons, his writing did not contain alphabet letters for a period of five months, even though he had created letters, and had used them for writing, during an earlier period.

APPENDIX C

Problems Encountered by a Child Whose Literacy Development Was More Advanced Than Her Kindergarten Peers

The story of what happened to one child who didn't fit the norm illustrates the importance of teaching from a coherent framework.

This kindergarten child began to read at home at the age of four without any specific tutoring from her parents. Her parents had read to her since she was very young, and she had access to many educational toys and materials. She was an only child whose parents usually found time to answer her questions and to play with her. They reported that she loved to write and read before she went to kindergarten.

She entered a public-school kindergarten at the age of five in a town considered to have progressive schools. Her kindergarten teacher had recently implemented a process-writing program and had incorporated daily writing

into the classroom schedule. The teacher had one firm rule about this writing period: The children were to do their own writing without help from the teacher. The teacher refused to answer any questions about spelling. Children were to do their own spelling, however they could do it. All efforts were accepted.

After several weeks of kindergarten, the child expressed a strong dislike for school in general, and for writing in particular. When she began to resist writing during writing periods in her classroom, one of her parents discussed the situation with the principal. It was decided that the language arts resource teacher would work with the child once or twice a week outside of the classroom. The language arts consultant would give the child more individual attention and would encourage her to relax and give up her perfectionism with respect to spelling. (According to the mother, the kindergarten teacher's goal for the year was to get this child to be less of a perfectionist.)

But the situation continued to deteriorate instead of improve, despite the added individual attention. The parents were advised to obtain a private psychological evaluation, which they did. The psychologist said the child was mildly depressed, which the teacher, the principal, and the language arts coordinator assumed was due to something in the family situation, such as unreasonable pressure for high academic performance. The mother claimed that the parents never did, and did not now, exert pressure. According to the mother, the child's problems centered around the teacher's approach to writing, particularly her refusal to answer the child's questions about spelling. This was the issue they needed to resolve with the school, and finally did.

While the explanations are rarely clear-cut and often involve many factors that interact to create the problem, I would like to suggest that the child's "perfectionism" only seemed to be a problem given the teacher's reference point, which was the typical kindergarten child. Most kindergarten children are perfectly happy to invent spellings. But they don't invent them because they are more willing to take risks, or because they feel free to be creative, or because they have no concern for perfection. They invent them because they don't know any better. They think their spellings are correct.

If adults simply provide spellings, without any other information, to a child who requests them, the child conceivably could become quite dependent on others for spellings. But if the adult uses the opportunity to help the child take the next conceptual step, the child can begin to see that spelling is hard because it isn't simply a matter of coding sounds heard. Once that occurs—once the child realizes that spelling involves a process that differs from strict phonetic coding—the child can begin to understand why independent spellings often don't match conventional ones. With the cognitive puzzle solved, the accompanying self-doubt often dissolves, and the child is often willing once again to invent spellings during the composing process and leave corrections for later editing. A child who doesn't realize that spelling is not a matter of strict phonetic coding can lose confidence in his or her own ability to create spellings; such a loss of confidence seems justified to me, under the circumstances. When this happens, children resort to asking for spellings instead of continuing to create spellings on their own. When their questions are ignored, they can become quite bewildered and frustrated.

After an initial phase of naive invented spelling, which is based on the assumption that spelling is a matter of strict phonetic transcription, children begin to realize that their own spellings do not match conventional forms. If they cling to their concept about how spelling is supposed to work while realizing at the same time that this approach doesn't yield spellings like those they see in books and the environment, they can experience considerable cognitive dissonance. This is not a particularly pleasant state, especially in a situation where the child is being made to do something while being deprived of the resources needed to resolve the puzzle. Most of us like to escape from such situations because they are extremely frustrating. When we can't, mild depression can result.

Furthermore, encouraging children not to pay attention to cognitive dissonance is a very poor practice. The strategies required for efficient studying and learning hinge on such things as realizing that there's a gap between your current level of understanding of something and complete understanding. It's this ability to monitor one's knowledge and thinking that psychologists are trying to understand (Harris et al. 1981; Flavell et al. 1987). Some children develop this ability, which is critical for such activities as efficient studying: If you don't know what you don't know, you can't use study time efficiently. Others have difficulty ever developing this ability to know what they know in relation to what's to be known. Perhaps children whose early attempts to resolve cognitive dissonance are ignored become some of the children who have difficulty later on. Luckily, due to the intervention of the kindergarten child's parents, she was able to resolve her cognitive dissonance and begin to enjoy school.

REFERENCES

Alegria, J., E. Pignot, and J. Morais. 1982. "Phonetic Analysis of Speech and Memory Codes in Beginning Readers." *Memory and Cognition* 10: 451–56.

Baghban, M. J. M. 1979. "Language Development and Initial Encounters with Written Language: A Case Study in Preschool Reading and Writing." Ph.D. diss., Indiana University.

Bissex, G. 1980. *GNYS AT WRK: A Child Learns to Write and Read*. Cambridge: Harvard University Press.

Brown, R. 1973. *A First Language*. Cambridge: Harvard University Press.

Clay, M. 1975. *What Did I Write? Beginning Writing Behaviour*. Portsmouth, NH: Heinemann.

———. 1983. "Getting a Theory of Writing." In *Explorations on the Development of Writing*, B. M. Kroll and G. Wells, eds. New York: John Wiley and Sons.

Dr. Seuss. 1961. *Dr. Seuss's ABC*. New York: Random House.

Durkin, D. 1966. *Children Who Read Early*. New York: Teachers College Press.

Ferreiro, E., and A. Teberosky. 1982. *Literacy before Schooling*. Trans. by K. G. Castro. Portsmouth, NH: Heinemann.

Flavell, J. H., J. R. Speer, F. L. Green, and D. L. Augrest. 1987. "The Development of Comprehension Monitoring and Knowledge about Comprehension." *Monographs for the Society for Research in Child Development*, serial no. 192, vol. 46.

Genishi, C., and A. H. Dyson. 1984. *Language Assessment in the Early Years*. Norwood, NJ: Ablex Publishing Corp.

Gentry, J. R. 1981. "Learning to Spell Developmentally." *The Reading Teacher* 35(2): 378–81.

———. 1982. "An Analysis of Developmental Spelling in GNYS AT WRK." *The Reading Teacher* 36(1): 192–200.

Hall, M., S. Moretz, and J. Statom. 1976. "A Study of Early Writing." *Language Arts* 53(5): 582—85.

Harris, P. L., A. Kruithf, M. M. Terwogt, and P. Visser. 1981. "Children's Detection and Awareness of Textual Anomaly." *Journal of Experimental Child Psychology* 31(1): 212—30.

Harste, J. C., C. L. Burke, and V. A. Woodward. 1981. *Children, Their Language and World: Initial Encounters with Print*. Final Report. Grant no. NIE-G-79-0132, National Institute of Education. Bloomington, IN: College of Education.

Heath, Shirley Brice. 1982. *Ways with Words: Language, Life, and Word in Communities and Classrooms*. New York: Cambridge University Press.

Henderson, E. H., and J. W. Beers. 1980. *Developmental and Cognitive Aspects of Learning to Spell: A Reflection of Word Knowledge*. Newark, DE: International Reading Association.

Hunt, J. McV. 1965. *Intelligence and Experience*. New York: Ronald Press.

Kamii, C. 1985. *Young Children Reinvent Arithmetic*. New York: Teachers College Press.

Lavine, L. O. 1977. "Differentiation of Letterlike Forms in Prereading Children." *Developmental Psychology* 13(2): 89—94.

Liberman, I., D. Shankweiler, F. Fischer, and B. Carter. 1974. "Explicit Syllable and Phoneme Segmentation in the Young Child." *Journal of Experimental Child Psychology* 18: 201—12.

McNeill, D. 1966. "Developmental Psycholinguistics." In *The Genesis of Language: A Psycholinguistic Approach*, 15—84, F. Smith and G. A. Miller, eds. Cambridge: MIT Press.

Mann, V. A. 1986. "Phonological Awareness: The Role of Reading Experience." *Cognition* 24(1): 65—92.

Papandropoulou, I., and H. Sinclair. 1974. "What's a Word? Experimental Study of Children's Ideas on Grammar." *Human Development* 17: 241—58.

Piaget, J. 1963. *The Origins of Intelligence in Children*. Trans. M. Cook. New York: W. W. Norton.

Pick, A. D., M. G. Unze, C. A. Brownell, J. G. Drozdal, and M. R. Hopmann. 1979. "Young Children's Knowledge of Word Structure." *Child Development* 49(3): 669—80.

Read, C. 1975. *Children's Categorization of Speech Sounds in English*. Urbana, IL: National Council of Teachers of English.

Snow, C. 1983. "Literacy and Language: Relationships during the Preschool Years." *Harvard Educational Review* 53(2): 165—189.

Steffe, L. P., and P. Cobb. 1988. *Construction of Arithmetical Meanings and Strategies*. New York: Springer-Verlag.

Sulzby, E. 1985. "Children's Emergent Reading of Favorite Storybooks." *Reading Research Quarterly* 20(4): 458—81.

Sulzby, E., and W. Teale. 1985. "Writing Development in Early Childhood." *Educational Horizons* 64(1): 8—12.

Vygotsky, L. S. 1978. *Mind in Society: The Development of Psychological Processes*. Cambridge: Harvard University Press.

Wells, G. 1986. *The Meaning Makers: Children Learning Language and Using Language to Learn*. Portsmouth, NH: Heinemann.

Wood, M. 1989. "Invented Spelling Revisited." *Reading Today* 6(6) (June/July): 22.

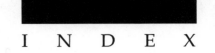